Laboratory Manual

CONCEPTS AND CHALLENGES

PHYSICAL ❖ SCIENCE

Martin Schachter ◆ Alan Winkler ◆ Stanley Wolfe

Stanley Wolfe
Project Coordinator

GLOBE FEARON
Pearson Learning Group

The following people have contributed to the development of this product:

Art and Design: Evelyn Bauer, Susan Brorein, Tracey Gerber, Bernadette Hruby, Carol Marie Kiernan, Mindy Klarman, Judy Mahoney, Karen Mancinelli, Elbaliz Mendez, April Okano, Dan Thomas, Jennifer Visco

Editorial: Stephanie P. Cahill, Gina Dalessio, Nija Dixon, Martha Feehan, Theresa McCarthy, Maurice Sabean, Marilyn Sarch, Maury Solomon, S. Adrienn Vegh-Soti, Shirley C. White, Jeffrey Wickersty

Manufacturing: Mark Cirillo, Tom Dunne

Marketing: Douglas Falk, Stephanie Schuler

Production: Irene Belinsky, Linda Bierniak, Carlos Blas, Karen Edmonds, Cheryl Golding, Leslie Greenberg, Roxanne Knoll, Susan Levine, Cynthia Lynch, Jennifer Murphy, Lisa Svoronos, Susan Tamm

Publishing Operations: Carolyn Coyle, Thomas Daning, Richetta Lobban

Technology: Ellen Strain

About the Cover: Physical science is the study of both physics and chemistry. The roller coaster and the spaceship on the cover illustrate examples of these concepts. The roller coaster represents the study of forces and motion. The spaceship, as it is lifting off, represents the chemistry that goes into creating the right mix of fuels. These concepts are just a few of the many things you will be learning about in this book. What do you think are some other things that you will study in physical science?

Globe Fearon
Pearson Learning Group

1-800-321-3106
www.pearsonlearning.com

CONTENTS

SAFETY IN THE SCIENCE LABORATORY

Unlike many other fields of study, science allows you an opportunity to "learn by doing." Part of this process often involves work both in the laboratory and in the field.

Working a science laboratory can be both exciting and meaningful. However, when carrying out experiments, you may sometimes work with materials that can be dangerous if not handled properly. For this reason, you must always be aware of proper safety procedures. You can avoid accidents in the laboratory by following a few simple guidelines:

- **Always** handle all material carefully.
- **Never** perform a laboratory investigation without direction from your teacher.
- **Never** work alone in the science laboratory.
- **Always** read directions in a laboratory investigation before beginning the laboratory.

Throughout this laboratory program, you will see the safety symbols that are shown below and on the next page. Before beginning any laboratory, be sure to read the laboratory and note any safety symbols and caution statements. If you know what each symbol means, and always follow the guidelines that apply to each symbol, your work in the laboratory will be both safe and exciting.

SAFETY SYMBOLS

Clothing Protection
- Wear your laboratory apron to protect your clothing from stains or burns.

Eye Safety
- Wear your laboratory goggles, especially when working with open flames and chemicals.
- If chemicals get into your eyes, flush your eyes with plenty of water. Notify your teacher immediately.
- Be sure you know how to use the emergency eyewash system in the laboratory.

Clean Up
- Always wash your hands after an activity in which you handle chemicals, animals, or plants.

Disposal
- Keep your work area clean at all times.
- Dispose of all materials properly. Follow your teacher's instructions for disposal.

Glassware Safety
- Handle glassware carefully.
- Check all glassware for chips or cracks before using it. Never use glassware that has chips or cracks.
- Do not try to clean up broken glassware. Notify your teacher if you break a piece of glassware.
- Air-dry all glassware. Do not use paper towels to dry glassware.
- Never force glass tubing into the hole of a rubber stopper.

Heating Safety
- Be careful when handling hot objects.
- Turn off the hot plate or other heat source when you are not using it.
- When you heat chemicals in a test tube, always point the test tube away from people.

Fire Safety
- Confine loose clothing and tie back long hair when working near an open flame.
- Be sure you know the location of fire extinguishers and fire blankets in the laboratory.
- Never reach across an open flame.

Dangerous Chemicals
- Use extreme care when working with acids and bases. Both acids and bases can cause burns. If you spill an acid or a base on your skin, flush your skin with plenty of water. Notify your teacher immediately.
- Never mix chemicals unless you are instructed to do so by your teacher.
- Never pour water into an acid or a base. Always pour an acid or a base into water.
- Never smell anything directly.
- Use caution when handling chemicals that produce fumes.

Poison
- Never use chemicals without directions from your teacher.
- Use all poisonous chemicals with extreme caution.
- Inform your teacher immediately if you spill chemicals or get any chemicals in your eyes or on your skin.

Sharp Objects
- Be careful when using scissors, scalpels, knives, or other cutting instruments.
- Always dissect specimens in a dissecting pan. Never dissect a specimen while holding it in your hand.
- Always cut in the direction away from your body.

Electrical Safety
- Check all electrical equipment for loose plugs or worn cords before using it.
- Be sure that electrical cords are not placed where people can trip over them.
- Do not use electrical equipment with wet hands or near water.
- Never overload an electrical circuit.

Plant Safety
- Never eat any part of a plant that you cannot identify as edible.
- Some plants, such as poison ivy, are harmful if they are touched or eaten. Use caution when handling or collecting plants. Always use a reliable field guide to plants.

Animal Safety
- Be careful when handling live animals. Some animals can injure you or spread disease.
- Do not bring live animals into class that have not been purchased from a reputable pet store.

Caution
- Follow the ⚠ CAUTION and safety symbols you see used throughout this manual when doing labs or other activities.

PHYSICAL SCIENCE EQUIPMENT AND APPARATUS

As you work in the physical science laboratory, you will need to become familiar with many pieces of equipment and apparatus. Several common pieces of equipment are shown below and on the next page. Below the name of each piece of equipment is a brief description of what the equipment is used for.

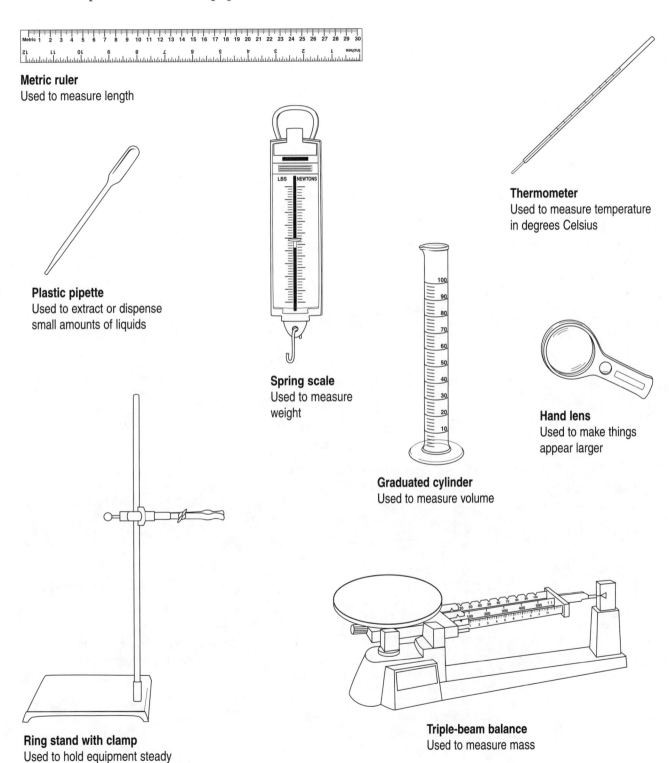

Metric ruler
Used to measure length

Plastic pipette
Used to extract or dispense small amounts of liquids

Spring scale
Used to measure weight

Thermometer
Used to measure temperature in degrees Celsius

Hand lens
Used to make things appear larger

Graduated cylinder
Used to measure volume

Ring stand with clamp
Used to hold equipment steady

Triple-beam balance
Used to measure mass

PHYSICAL SCIENCE EQUIPMENT AND APPARATUS

Funnel and filter paper
Used to separate mixtures

Dry cells
Used to produce an electric current

Stirring rod
Used to mix materials

Dropper
Used to add small amounts of liquids

Tongs
Used to grasp objects

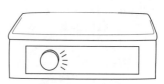

Hot plate
Used to heat materials

Beakers
Used to hold materials

Test tube holder
Used to hold hot test tubes

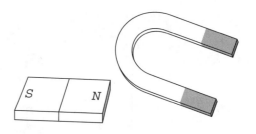

Magnets
Used to produce a magnetic field and to attract objects containing iron

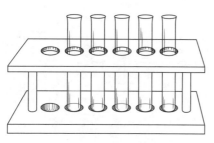

Test tubes and rack
Used to hold materials

Name _____ Class _____ Date _____

LABORATORY SKILLS WORKSHEET 1

Using a Graduated Cylinder

Materials

100-mL graduated
cylinder

dropper

small jar

BACKGROUND: A graduated cylinder is used to measure the volume of a liquid. A graduated cylinder is a long tube marked along its side with lines that show the volume. Some graduated cylinders are small and measure only up to 10 milliliters of liquid. Others are larger and measure 25 milliliters, 100 milliliters, or more. Notice the 10-milliliter graduated cylinder in Figure 1. The long lines below the numbers show milliliters. The shorter lines show two-tenths of a milliliter. Other graduated cylinders may have different values for the long and short lines. When you pour a liquid into a graduated cylinder, you can use these lines to determine the volume of the liquid.

PURPOSE: In this activity, you will learn how to use a graduated cylinder.

▲ Figure 1 A 10-mL graduated cylinder

PROCEDURE 🔬

Part A: Reading a Graduated Cylinder

❑ 1. **OBSERVE:** Look at a graduated cylinder. Notice the markings on the side. The markings on a graduated cylinder are usually given in milliliters, which is abbreviated mL. Record information about this graduated cylinder in Table 1 on page 6.

❑ 2. Look at the graduated cylinder shown in Figure 2. Notice that the surface of the liquid is curved upward at the sides. This curve is called a meniscus. When you read the volume of a liquid in a graduated cylinder, you must look at it from eye level. Always read the volume at the flat, center part of the meniscus. In Figure 2, the volume is 8.6 mL.

❑ 3. Look at the graduated cylinder readings in Figure 3. Write the volume of the liquid in each graduated cylinder in the space provided.

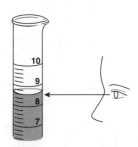

▲ Figure 2 Reading the meniscus of a liquid in a graduated cylinder

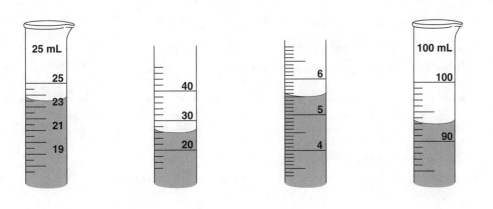

1. _____   2. _____   3. _____   4. _____

▲ Figure 3 Write the volume of liquid in each graduated cylinder.

Part B: Measuring the Volume of a Liquid

❏ 1. **MEASURE:** Half fill a small jar with water. Pour the water into the graduated cylinder. Record the volume of the water in Table 2. Ask your teacher to check your answer. Empty your graduated cylinder.

❏ 2. Repeat Step 4 two more times. Have your lab partner check your answers.

❏ 3. **MEASURE:** Use a graduated cylinder to measure 64 mL of water. First, fill the jar with water. Pour water from the jar into the graduated cylinder until it is between the 60 and 70-mL mark. Look at the meniscus from eye level. If the reading is greater than 64 mL, pour some of the water back into the jar. If the reading is less than 64 mL, use a dropper to get water from the jar and add it to the graduated cylinder. Continue until the lower part of the meniscus is on the 64-mL line.

❏ 4. Repeat Step 3 to measure 82 mL and 93 mL. Have your lab partner check your readings each time.

OBSERVATIONS

Table 1: Information About the Graduated Cylinder	
Greatest volume it will measure	
Volume shown by the longest lines	
Volume shown by the shortest lines	

Table 2: Reading a Graduated Cylinder	
Volume 1	
Volume 2	
Volume 3	

CONCLUSIONS

1. **COMPARE:** What is an advantage of measuring a liquid with a graduated cylinder

instead of a beaker? _____

_____

2. **INFER:** If the smallest markings on a graduated cylinder are 1 mL apart, is it possible to measure a volume of 63.5 mL? Explain your answer.

_____

_____

3. Suppose that the long markings on a graduated cylinder are 1 mL apart and there are four short lines between the 8-mL and the 9-mL marks. What volumes do the short lines indicate?

_____

_____

Name _____ Class _____ Date _____

LABORATORY SKILLS WORKSHEET 2

Using a Triple-Beam Balance

Materials

solid object

beaker

salt

tablespoon

triple-beam balance

BACKGROUND: Triple-beam balances are often used to find the mass of solid objects or powdered solids. Most triple-beam balances have a balance pan, three beams, a pointer, and a three-part scale with riders. Many balances also have an adjustment knob. The scale of a balance measures grams. The scale of the top beam gives readings in 10-gram intervals, for example, 10 grams, 20 grams, and so on, up to 100 grams. The scale of the middle beam gives readings in hundreds of grams. The scale of the bottom beam gives readings in grams from 1 gram to 10 grams. Each 1-gram interval shows tenths of a gram, from 0.1 gram to 0.9 gram. A triple-beam balance measures the mass of an object by balancing the mass in the pan with the riders on the scale.

PURPOSE: In this activity, you will learn how to use a triple-beam balance.

Pan · Riders · Scale · Pointer · Adjustment knob

PROCEDURE

Part A: Reading a Mass

❏ 1. To read the mass of an object, read the position of the hundreds, tens, and ones riders to find the mass in hundreds, tens, ones, and tenths of grams. Read the mass shown on the triple-beam balance scale below.

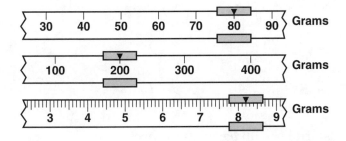

30 40 50 60 70 80 90 〉 Grams

100 200 300 400 〉 Grams

3 4 5 6 7 8 9 〉 Grams

Table 1: Reading a Mass	
Rider	**Mass**
Tens rider	
Hundreds rider	
Ones rider	
Total mass	

❏ 2. **RECORD:** Record the mass shown by each rider in Table 1. Make sure that you write a decimal point before the number of tenths shown on the ones rider.

❏ 3. Add the masses together to find the total mass. Record this in Table 1.

Part B: Finding the Mass of a Solid Object

❏ 1. Before using a triple-beam balance, make sure that the balance is centered properly. Set all the riders to zero. The balance pointer should rest at the zero mark at the end of the scale. If the balance pointer is not at zero, turn the adjustment knob until the pointer arrives at zero.

❏ **2.** Place the object on the balance pan.

❏ **3.** **MEASURE:** Slide the riders until the pointer is once again on zero. This means that the scale is balanced. If the mass of the object is less than 10 grams, you will find that you do not need to move the top rider. If the mass of the object is less than 100 grams, you will not need to move the middle rider.

❏ **4.** **RECORD:** To find the mass of the object, first record the measurement shown on each of the three riders. Record this information in Table 2. Then, add the masses of each rider to find the total mass. Record your measurement in Table 2.

Part C: Finding the Mass of a Substance

❏ **1.** **MODEL:** Place a beaker on the balance pan to find its mass. Record this mass in Table 3.

❏ **2.** **MEASURE:** Place 1 tablespoon of salt in the beaker. Find the mass of the beaker and the salt combined. Record the mass in Table 3.

❏ **3.** **CALCULATE:** To find the mass of the salt alone, subtract the mass of the beaker from the combined mass of the beaker and salt. Record the mass of the salt in Table 3.

OBSERVATIONS

Table 2: Reading a Mass	
Rider	Mass
Tens rider	
Hundreds rider	
Ones rider	
Total mass	

Table 3: Finding the Mass of a Substance	
Mass of beaker (a)	
Mass of beaker plus salt (b)	
Total mass (b minus a)	

CONCLUSIONS

1. **CALCULATE:** What is the greatest mass that most triple-beam balances can accurately measure? _____

2. **INFER:** If only the ones rider needs to be moved from zero to balance a mass on the the balance pan, what is the largest mass that the object can have? _____

3. **INFER:** If the hundreds rider is left at zero and the tens and ones riders are moved to balance the scale, what is the largest mass that the object in the balance pan can have?

_____

Concepts and Challenges in Physical Science, Laboratory Manual © Pearson Education, Inc./Globe Fearon/Pearson Learning Group. All rights reserved. Copying strictly prohibited.

LABORATORY SKILLS WORKSHEET 3

Measuring Volume and Density

BACKGROUND: When you blow up a balloon, you force air into the balloon. The volume of the balloon must increase because the air takes up space. Volume is the amount of space that matter takes up. If you hold the balloon in one hand and hold a ball of the same size in your other hand, you notice that the ball is heavier. This is because the density of the ball is greater than that of the balloon. Density is the amount of matter in a given volume.

PURPOSE: In this activity, you will learn how to measure the volumes and densities of different solids and liquids.

PROCEDURE

Part A: Mass and Volume of a Rectangular Solid

❑ 1. Use a metric ruler to measure the length, width, and height of a wooden block. Use a wax pencil to label this block *1*. Record your measurements in Table 1 on page 11.

❑ 2. **CALCULATE:** Calculate the volume of block 1, using the following formula.

Volume = length × width × height

Record the volume in Table 1 and in Table 3.

❑ 3. Label the other wooden block *2*. Label the remaining rectangular solids *3* and *4*. In the spaces provided in Tables 1 and 3, indicate what materials solids 3 and 4 are made of.

❑ 4. Repeat Steps 1 and 2 for wooden block 2 and for solids 3 and 4.

❑ 5. Use a triple-beam balance to measure the masses of the wooden blocks and the other rectangular solids. Record the measurements in Table 3.

Part B: Mass and Volume of a Liquid

❑ 1. **MEASURE:** Use the balance to measure the mass of an empty 150-mL beaker. Record the measurement here.

mass of beaker = _____ g

❑ 2. **MEASURE:** Half fill the beaker with water. Place it on the balance and measure the mass of the beaker and water together. Find the mass of the water, using the following formula.

Mass (water) = mass (beaker + water) − mass (beaker)

Record the mass of the water in Table 3.

Materials

100-mL graduated cylinder

150-mL beaker

2 rectangular solids of the same dimensions but different materials

2 rectangular wooden blocks of different dimensions

rubbing alcohol

wax pencil

metric ruler

small rock

triple-beam balance

❏ 3. Pour the water from the beaker into the graduated cylinder. Measure the volume of the water. Remember to read the volume by looking at the bottom of the meniscus. Record the measurement in Table 3.

❏ 4. Empty the graduated cylinder. Pour the same amount of rubbing alcohol as you had water into the graduated cylinder. Record the volume of rubbing alcohol in Table 3.

❏ 5. Pour the rubbing alcohol into the beaker. Use the balance to measure the mass of the rubbing alcohol and beaker together. Use the formula in Step 2 to find the mass of the rubbing alcohol. Record the mass of the alcohol in Table 3.

Part C: Mass and Volume of an Irregular Solid

❏ 1. Half fill the graduated cylinder with water. Read the volume of the water. Record the measurement in Table 2.

❏ 2. Carefully lower a small rock into the water in the graduated cylinder. The water level should rise. Read the level of the water. Record the volume of the water and rock in Table 2.

❏ 3. Find the volume of the rock, using the following formula.

Volume (rock) = volume (water + rock) – volume (water)

Because 1 mL = 1 cm^3, you can express the volume of the rock in cm^3.

❏ 4. Record the volume of the rock in Table 2 and Table 3.

❏ 5. Use the balance to find the mass of the rock. Record the mass in Table 3.

Part D: Density

❏ 1. **CALCULATE:** Calculate the density of wooden block 1, using the following formula.

Density = mass (g) ÷ volume (cm^3)

Record the density in Table 3.

❏ 2. Repeat Step 1 for wooden block 2, rectangular solids 3 and 4, and the rock.

❏ 3. Calculate the density of water, using the following formula.

Density = mass (g) ÷ volume (mL)

Record the density in Table 3.

❏ 4. Repeat Step 3 for the rubbing alcohol.

Name _____ Class _____ Date _____

LABORATORY SKILLS WORKSHEET 3 (continued)

OBSERVATIONS

Table 1: Volumes of Rectangular Solids				
Item	**Length**	**Width**	**Height**	**Volume**
Wooden block 1				cm³
Wooden block 2				cm³
Solid 3 _____				cm³
Solid 4 _____				cm³

Table 2: Volume of an Irregular Solid	
Object	**Volume**
Water	_____ mL
Water + rock	_____ mL
Rock alone	_____ mL = _____ cm³

Table 3: Mass, Volume, and Density			
Substance	**Mass**	**Volume**	**Density**
Wooden block 1	g	cm³	g/cm³
Wooden block 2	g	cm³	g/cm³
Solid 3 _____	g	cm³	g/cm³
Solid 4 _____	g	cm³	g/cm³
Water	g	cm³	g/cm³
Rubbing alcohol	g	cm³	g/cm³
Rock	g	cm³	g/cm³

1. Which wooden block has the greater volume? Which has the greater mass?

   _____

2. How do the densities of the two wooden blocks compare? _____

   _____

3. Which rectangular solid—3 or 4—has the greater density? _____

4. Which liquid—water or rubbing alcohol—has the greater density? _____

CONCLUSIONS

5. How is the volume of a rectangular solid measured? _____

   _____

6. How is the volume of a liquid measured? _____

   _____

7. How is the volume of an irregular solid measured? Why is this method necessary?

   _____

   _____

   _____

8. Can two solids with the same volume have different densities? Explain your

   answer. _____

   _____

9. Can two solids made of the same substance have different densities? Explain

   your answer. _____

   _____

10. **COMPARE:** If you filled a 1-L bottle with water and another 1-L bottle with rubbing

    alcohol, which bottle would feel heavier? Why? _____

    _____

    _____

LABORATORY SKILLS WORKSHEET 4

Organizing and Analyzing Data

Materials

paper
pencil

BACKGROUND: Data collected during experiments is not very useful unless it is easy to read and understand. Therefore, scientists often use tables to organize data. A table can display a lot of information in a small space. A table also makes it easy to compare and interpret data. Some tables, such as the one in Figure 1, are very simple and show only a small amount of data. Other tables, such as the one on page 14, are more complex. The type of table you use depends on your data.

PURPOSE: In this activity, you will learn how to make and use tables.

Object	Volume (cm³)
1	48.2
2	31.6
3	51.9

▲ **Figure 1** A simple table

PROCEDURE

❏ **1.** During an experiment, students measured the amount of force required to pull four different blocks up a ramp. For the first measurement, they positioned the ramp so that it made a 10° angle with the ground. Then they raised the ramp to a 20° angle, a 30° angle, and a 40° angle to see how the force required to pull the block changed. They repeated these measurements for each of the remaining blocks. Figure 2 shows what one student's lab manual looked like after recording the measurements. Think about how this data could be organized into a table.

❏ **2. ORGANIZE:** Look at Table 1 on page 14. Like all tables, it has a title. Each column has a heading, and the headings show units for the data. Use the data from the student's lab manual in Figure 2 to complete the table. Since the units are already given, do not write the unit abbreviation beside each measurement you record.

Lab Manual

○ <u>Block 1</u>
10°, 0.9 N; 20°, 1.5 N; 30°, 2.2 N; 40°, 2.8 N

<u>Block 2</u>
10°, 0.5 N; 20°, 0.9 N; 30°, 1.4 N; 40°, 1.8 N

<u>Block 3</u>
10°, 1.0 N; 20°, 1.8 N; 30°, 2.7 N; 40°, 3.5 N

<u>Block 4</u>
○ 10°, 0.8 N; 20°, 1.3 N; 30°, 2.0 N; 40°, 2.5 N

▲ **Figure 2** A student collected this data.

OBSERVATIONS

Table 1: Movement of Blocks Up a Ramp				
	Force (newtons)			
Ramp Angle	Block 1	Block 2	Block 3	Block 4
10°				
20°				
30°				
40°				

1. How much did the force required to move Block 1 change when the ramp was raised from an angle of 10° to an angle of 20°?

   _____

2. How much did the force required to move Block 3 change when the ramp was raised from an angle of 20° to an angle of 30°?

   _____

3. How much more force was required to pull Block 2 up a ramp placed at an

   angle of 30° than to pull Block 4 up a ramp placed at an angle of 20°? _____

4. Which block required the most force to pull up a ramp placed at an angle of 40°? _____

5. Which block required the least force to pull up a ramp placed at an angle of 10°? _____

CONCLUSIONS

6. **PREDICTING:** Approximately what force would probably be required to pull Block 3

   and Block 4 up a ramp placed at an angle of 30° at the same time? _____

7. **ANALYZING:** Which of the blocks used in the experiment probably weighed the most?

   How do you know? _____

8. **COMPARING:** Look at how the data was written in Figure 2 and how it was displayed in the table you completed. Explain how the table makes it easier to understand the data.

   _____

9. **ORGANIZE:** Look again at the data shown in the student's lab manual in Figure 2. How would the table look if the student had measured the force required to move one block instead of four? On a separate sheet of paper, make a table that students could use to present their data.

   _____

Concepts and Challenges in Physical Science, Laboratory Manual © Pearson Education, Inc./Globe Fearon/Pearson Learning Group. All rights reserved. Copying strictly prohibited.

LABORATORY SKILLS WORKSHEET 5

Graphing

BACKGROUND: Graphs are a useful way to organize and present information. Graphing data helps you see similarities and patterns. It also helps other people understand your data. Four types of graphs you may use are line graphs, bar graphs, circle graphs, and pictographs.

PURPOSE: In this activity, you will learn to make different kinds of graphs.

PROCEDURE

Part A: Making a Line Graph

Changes in Car Speed

(graph showing Speed (km/h) vs Time (s))

▲ **Figure 1** Line graph

❏ 1. **OBSERVE:** Look at the line graph in Figure 1. Notice that data are plotted as points connected by a line. The horizontal axis shows the range of the independent variable. The vertical axis shows the range of the dependent variable. When graphing, you must decide which values are independent and which are dependent. In Figure 1, the speed of the car depends on the time. Therefore, the speed is the dependent variable, which goes on the vertical axis. The time goes on the horizontal axis.

❏ 2. **GRAPH:** Use the following information to create your own line graph in the Observations section on page 17.

> A student measured changes in the temperature of water as it was heated. The beginning temperature of the water (in degrees Celsius) was 36°. The temperature then rose to 42° after 1 minute, 50° after 2 minutes, 60° after 3 minutes, 70° after 4 minutes, 79° after 5 minutes, 88° after 6 minutes, 97° after 7 minutes, and 100° after 8 minutes.

Think about which variable is independent and which is dependent. Remember to include a title and to label the axes. Notice that the low temperature is 36° and the high is 100°. The temperature range on your graph should be from just below this number to just above it.

Part B: Making a Bar Graph

❏ 1. **OBSERVE:** Figure 2 shows a bar graph using the same data as in Figure 1. A bar graph is similar to a line graph except bars rather than points show the data. The bar graph in Figure 2 has the dependent variable on the vertical axis. Bar graphs may also be drawn so that the dependent variable is on the horizontal axis.

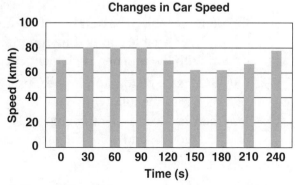

Changes in Car Speed

▲ **Figure 2** Bar graph

❑ 2. **GRAPH:** Use the information about increase in water temperature given in Part A Step 2 to create a bar graph in the Observations section. Be sure to label the axes of the graph and to include a title.

Part C: Making a Circle Graph

❑ 1. **OBSERVE:** Look at the circle graph shown in Figure 3. You can use a circle graph when your data describe parts of a whole. A circle graph is a circle that is divided into sections. The size of each section shows a percentage of the whole circle. Notice that if you add the percentages of the sections together, they equal 100 percent.

❑ 2. If the data are simple, you can draw a circle graph based on simple fractions of a whole. Suppose you want to graph the number of atoms contained in each molecule of a substance having the chemical formula $C_2H_2F_4$. The formula shows that each molecule has 8 atoms: 2 carbon atoms, 2 hydrogen atoms, and 4 fluorine atoms. Since 2 is 1/4 of the total number of atoms, and 4 is 1/2 the total number of atoms, your graph should look like Figure 4.

❑ 3. **GRAPH:** A group of students classified 24 objects according to the kinds of simple machines they were. They identified 6 inclined planes, 8 levers, 6 pulleys, and 4 wheel and axles. Draw a circle graph in the Observations section showing this information. Fill in the four sections using colored pencils to make the graph easier to read. Label the sections and write a title for the graph.

Part D: Making a Pictograph

❑ 1. **OBSERVE:** As the name suggests, a pictograph is a graph using pictures. Look at the pictograph in Figure 5. The percentages of the elements are represented by the amount of space they occupy on the picture. Figure 6 shows another type of pictograph. In this graph, small pictures show the classification of elements on the periodic table. The number of elements in each category is the dependent variable and is drawn horizontally. The graph could also be drawn with the number of elements in each category drawn vertically.

❑ 2. **GRAPH:** Make a pictograph in the Observations section showing the results of a race. Use the following data for your graph: 2 students ran the race in less than 10 seconds, 7 ran between 11 and 12 seconds, 12 ran between 12 and 15 seconds, and 4 ran the race in more than 15 seconds. Remember to include a title.

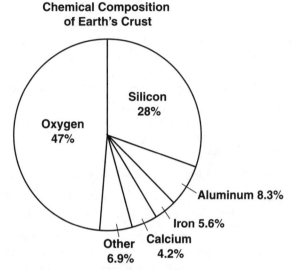

Chemical Composition of Earth's Crust

▲ **Figure 3** Circle graph using percentages

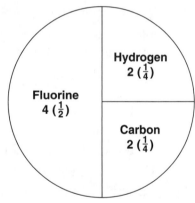

Atoms in Molecule of $C_2H_2F_4$

▲ **Figure 4** Circle graph using fractions

LABORATORY SKILLS WORKSHEET 5 *(continued)*

**Percentages of Elements in
Methylene Blue Solution
(by mass)**

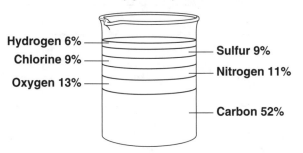

Hydrogen 6%
Chlorine 9%
Oxygen 13%

Sulfur 9%
Nitrogen 11%
Carbon 52%

▲ **Figure 5** Pictograph showing percentages

**Classification of Elements
on the Periodic Table**

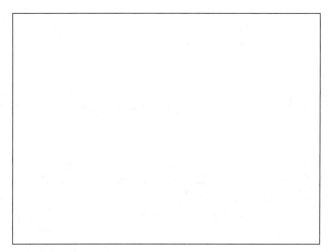

▲ **Figure 6** Pictograph based on numbers

OBSERVATIONS

▲ **Line Graph**

▲ **Bar Graph**

▲ **Circle Graph**

▲ **Pictograph**

CONCLUSIONS

1. What information is presented in the line graph shown in Figure 1? _____
   _____

2. What information is presented along the horizontal axis of Figure 1? _____
   _____

3. What information is presented along the vertical axis of Figure 2? _____

4. What is the independent variable in Figure 2? What is the dependent variable
   in Figure 2? _____

5. Look at the line graph in Figure 1. What trend do you see in the speed of the car?
   _____

6. How does the bar graph in Figure 2 show this same trend? _____
   _____

7. How would the bar graph shown in Figure 2 look different if the independent
   variable was on the vertical axis instead of on the horizontal axis?
   _____

8. Use the line graph in Figure 1 to determine the speed of the car after it had
   traveled 2 minutes. _____

9. What information is shown in the circle graph in Figure 3? _____

10. According to Figure 3, what element makes up most of Earth's crust? What
    percent of the crust is made up of this element? _____

11. According to Figure 3, what is the combined percentage of aluminum and iron? _____

12. How does a pictograph make data easier to understand compared to using
    only numbers? _____
    _____

LABORATORY SKILLS WORKSHEET 6

Writing a Laboratory Report

Materials

pencil

BACKGROUND: When you perform a laboratory investigation, it is important to keep an organized record of what you do. It is also important to keep an accurate record of your results. An organized record of an investigation is called a laboratory report. A laboratory report is made up of the following sections: Title, Purpose, Background, Hypothesis, Materials, Procedure, Observations, Data, Analysis of Data, and Conclusions.

PURPOSE: In this activity, you will learn how to write a laboratory report.

PROCEDURE

❏ 1. Study the following descriptions of the sections of a laboratory report.

Title—tells about the experiment
Purpose—reason for doing the experiment
Background—information that will help a reader understand the experiment better
Hypothesis—your idea on what you expect the results of the experiment to be
Materials—list of things needed to perform the experiment
Procedure—steps that will be followed during the experiment
Observations—description of what is seen during the experiment
Data—measurements made during the experiment
Analysis of Data—presentation of the data in tables, charts, graphs, or drawings
Conclusions—summary statement of the results; describes whether the data supported the hypothesis and sources of any errors

> Two students thought that the mechanical advantage of a single fixed pulley was 2. To check, they used a 2-kg mass, a spring scale, a rope, and a single fixed pulley. First, they used the spring scale to find how much force was needed to lift the mass. Then, they attached the mass to one end of the rope and passed the other end over the fixed pulley. They attached this end of the rope to the spring scale. By pulling down on the spring scale, they were able to find the effort force needed to lift the mass. They then compared this force with the force needed to lift the mass without the pulley. They found that the pulley did not change the effort force. They concluded that the mechanical advantage of the fixed pulley was equal to 1.

❏ 2. Reread the experiment described above. Write a possible title for the experiment.

_____

❏ 3. Notice the data that the students obtained in the experiment. Make a table to record data for the experiment in the Observations section on page 20.

LABORATORY SKILLS WORKSHEET 6 *(continued)*

OBSERVATIONS

CONCLUSIONS

1. State the purpose of this experiment in the form of a question. _____
_____

2. What was the hypothesis in this experiment? _____
_____

3. Make a list of materials that the students needed to carry out this experiment.
_____
_____

4. What variable was being tested in this experiment? _____
_____
_____

5. Write a step-by-step procedure for this experiment. _____
_____
_____
_____
_____

6. Write the conclusion that students reached based on their results. _____
_____

Name _____ Class _____ Date _____

LABORATORY CHALLENGE FOR LESSON 1-4

What happens during a change of state?

BACKGROUND: Most matter on Earth commonly exists in any of three familiar states: solid, liquid, or gas. In a solid, particles vibrate about a fixed position. Solid substances have a definite shape because particles are tightly packed together. Particles of a liquid are loosely connected. Liquid substances cannot hold their shape on their own. Particles of a gas are not connected at all. Gas particles are widely separated. In order for a substance to experience a change of state, energy must be added to or removed from the substance.

PURPOSE: In this activity, you will observe what happens when a substance changes state.

> ## Materials
>
> safety goggles
> lab apron
> heat source
> ring stand
> thermometer clamp
> stirring rod
> 250-mL beaker, filled to the 200-mL mark with crushed ice
> thermometer
> graph paper
> clock or watch

PROCEDURE

☐ 1. Put on safety goggles and a lab apron.

☐ 2. Assemble the ring stand, thermometer clamp, and thermometer as shown in Figure 1.

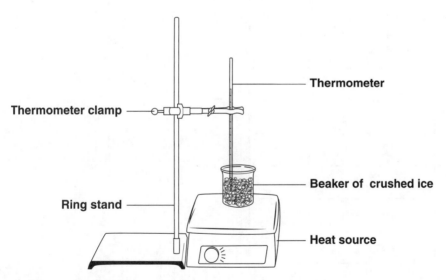

▲ **Figure 1** Attach the thermometer and clamp to the ring stand.

☐ 3. Place a beaker of finely crushed ice on the heat source.

☐ 4. Lower a thermometer into the crushed ice. Do not let the thermometer touch the sides or the bottom of the beaker.

☐ 5. **MEASURE:** Use the thermometer to measure the temperature of the crushed ice. Record the temperature in the box for 0 min in Table 1 on page 22.

❑ 6. Turn on the heat source so that the crushed ice begins to heat. Do not readjust the setting. ⚠ CAUTION: **Always be careful when using a heat source. Never leave a heat source unattended.**

❑ 7. **OBSERVE:** After 1 min, observe the temperature of the ice-water mixture. Record the temperature in Table 1.

❑ 8. **OBSERVE:** Repeat Step 7 every min for 15 min. Stir the ice-water mixture just before taking the temperature each time.

❑ 9. Circle the temperature and the time when the ice is completely melted. Circle the temperature and the time when the first bubbles indicate boiling.

❑10. Follow your teacher's instructions for cleaning up your work area.

❑11. **ORGANIZE:** Organize your data by making a graph of temperature versus time. Use the graph paper in Figure 2. Put time on the horizontal axis, or *x*-axis, and temperature on the vertical axis, or *y*-axis. Plot and connect the points.

OBSERVATIONS

Table 1: Temperature Measurements			
Time (min)	Temp. (°C)	Time (min)	Temp (°C)
0		8	
1		9	
2		10	
3		11	
4		12	
5		13	
6		14	
7		15	

1. **DESCRIBE:** What happened to the temperature during the experiment?

_____

_____

_____

Name _____ Class _____ Date _____

LABORATORY CHALLENGE FOR LESSON 1-4 *(continued)*

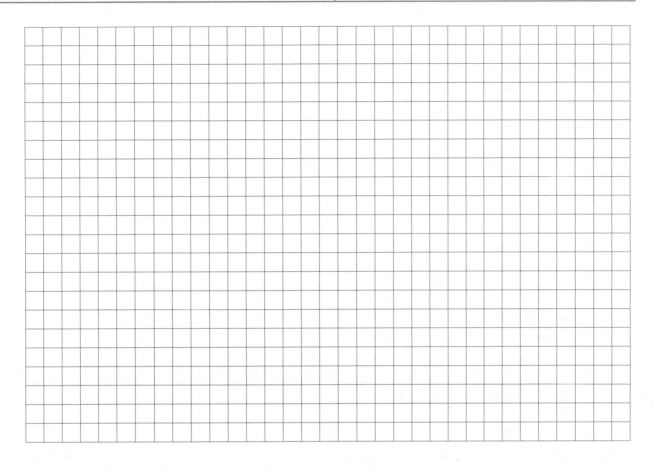

▲ **Figure 2** Graph paper

2. **DESCRIBE:** What is the shape of your graph? _____

_____

3. **ANALYZE:** What does the first flat region of the graph represent?

_____

_____

4. **ANALYZE:** What does the second flat region of the graph represent?

_____

_____

5. **COMMUNICATE:** How long did it take the water to start boiling?

_____

6. **COMMUNICATE:** What was the highest temperature recorded on your table? When was it recorded?

_____

CONCLUSIONS

7. **NAME:** In what familiar states can most matter exist? _____

8. **INFER:** What is required in order for a change in state to occur?

_____

CRITICAL THINKING

9. **DESCRIBE:** Based on your observations, describe how a sample of matter changed state during this experiment.

_____

_____

_____

_____

10. **ANALYZE:** During the experiment, the temperature of the ice-water mixture stayed the same for a brief period of time although it was being heated. Why?

_____

_____

11. **ANALYZE:** Which change requires more energy—ice to water or water to steam? How can you tell?

_____

_____

12. **HYPOTHESIZE:** How would your observations in this experiment change if the heat source was hotter?

_____

_____

_____

Name _____ Class _____ Date _____

How can you find the density of a substance?

Materials

safety goggles

lab apron

100-mL graduated
  cylinder

rectangular wooden
  block

triple-beam balance

metric ruler

100-mL beaker

small rock

BACKGROUND: Density tells you how much of a substance is in a certain amount of space. It is measured as mass per unit volume. Density is usually expressed as grams per cubic centimeter (g/cm^3). Since $1\ cm^3 = 1\ mL$, density can also be written as grams per milliliter (g/mL).

PURPOSE: In this activity, you will learn how to find the density of a liquid, a rectangular solid, and an irregular solid.

PROCEDURE

Part A: Density of a Liquid

☐ **1.** Put on safety goggles and a lab apron.

☐ **2.** **MEASURE:** Use a graduated cylinder to measure 75 mL of water, as shown in Figure 1. Record the volume of the water in Table 1 on page 27.

☐ **3.** **MEASURE:** Use the balance to find the mass of an empty 100-mL beaker. Record the mass below.

    mass of beaker = _____ g

☐ **4.** **CALCULATE:** Pour the 75 mL of water into the beaker and find the mass of the beaker and water. To find the mass of the water, use the following formula.

       mass of water = mass (beaker + water) – mass (beaker)

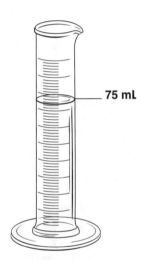

▲ **Figure 1** Measure 75 mL of water.

Record the mass of the water in Table 1.

☐ **5.** **CALCULATE:** Calculate the density of the water by using the following formula.

       density = mass (g) ÷ volume (mL)

Record the density of water in Table 1.

Part B: Density of a Rectangular Solid

❑ 1. **MEASURE:** Use the balance to find the mass of a rectangular wooden block. Record the mass in Table 1.

❑ 2. **MEASURE:** Measure the length, width, and height of the block in centimeters. Record your measurements below.

length = _____ cm

width = _____ cm

height = _____ cm

❑ 3. **CALCULATE:** Calculate the volume of the block, using the following formula.

volume = length × width × height

Record the volume of the block in Table 1.

❑ 4. **CALCULATE:** Calculate the density of the block, using the following formula.

density = mass (g) ÷ volume (cm³)

Record the density of the block in Table 1.

Part C: Density of an Irregular Solid

❑ 1. **MEASURE:** Use the balance to determine the mass of a small rock. Record the mass in Table 1.

❑ 2. Fill the graduated cylinder with water to the 50-mL mark.

❑ 3. **OBSERVE:** Tilt the graduated cylinder and gently lower the rock into the water, as shown in Figure 2. Observe the change in the height of the water. Record the new level of the water below.

water level = _____ mL

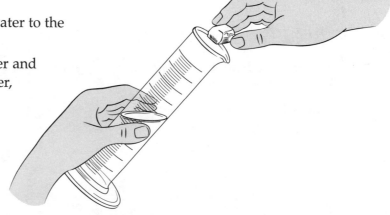

▲ **Figure 2** Tilt the graduated cylinder so that the rock slides in gently.

LABORATORY CHALLENGE FOR LESSON 2-2 *(continued)*

❑ **4. CALCULATE:** Find the volume of the rock, using the following formula.

volume of rock = water level (with submerged rock) – water level (without rock)

Since 1 mL = 1 cm³, you can express the volume of the rock in cubic centimeters. Record the volume of the rock in Table 1.

❑ **5. CALCULATE:** To calculate the density of the rock, use the same formula you used in Part B, Step 4. Record the density in Table 1.

❑ **6.** Follow your teacher's instructions to clean up your work area.

OBSERVATIONS

Table 1: Determining Density			
Item	**Volume**	**Mass**	**Density**
Water	mL	g	g/mL
Wooden block	cm³	g	g/cm³
Rock	cm³	g	g/cm³

CONCLUSIONS

1. DESCRIBE: How can you find the density of a liquid?

_____

_____

_____

_____

2. **DESCRIBE:** How can you find the density of a rectangular solid?

_____

_____

_____

_____

3. **DESCRIBE:** How can you find the density of an irregular solid?

_____

_____

_____

_____

CRITICAL THINKING

4. **APPLY:** If the wood block was cut into smaller pieces, how would the density of one of the smaller pieces compare to the density of the original block? Explain your answer.

_____

_____

_____

_____

Name _____ Class _____ Date _____

LABORATORY CHALLENGE FOR LESSON 3-8

How can you tell the difference between a metal and a nonmetal?

BACKGROUND: If you look at the periodic table, you will see a zigzag line separating the metals from the nonmetals. Metals and nonmetals often have opposite properties. For example, most metals can be bent, pounded, or pulled into other shapes. Most solid nonmetals, however, are brittle and easily broken.

PURPOSE: In this activity, you will learn how elements can be classified as metals or nonmetals.

PROCEDURE

❑ 1. Put on safety goggles and a lab apron.

❑ 2. Place each element sample on a separate piece of paper. Write the name of the element on the paper.

❑ 3. **OBSERVE:** Record the physical appearance of each element in Table 1 on page 31.

❑ 4. **OBSERVE:** Using the sample of carbon, touch the two leads of the conductivity tester to opposite sides of the sample. If the bulb lights, the element conducts an electric current. Record your observation by writing *yes* or *no* under "Electrical Conductivity" in Table 1.

Materials

safety goggles

lab apron

gloves

samples of

  carbon rod

  sulfur chunk

  copper

  aluminum

  iron

  lead

6 pieces of paper

pencil

conductivity tester

6 test tubes

test-tube brush

test-tube rack

dilute hydrochloric acid
  (10% solution)

paper towels

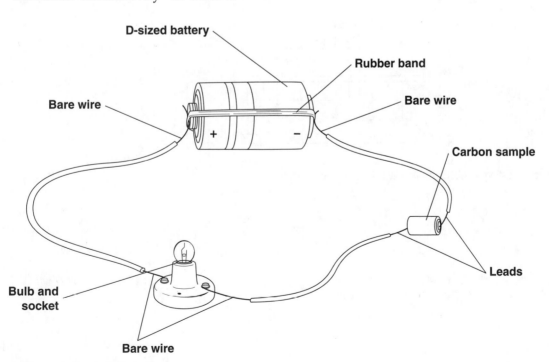

▲ **Figure 1** Conductivity tester

❑ **5.** Repeat Step 3 for each of the other element samples.

❑ **6.** Add a different element to each of the six test tubes. Ask your teacher to add a small amount of dilute hydrochloric acid to each test tube.

❑ **7.** **OBSERVE:** Watch for any change in the samples. If you see evidence of a chemical change, write *yes* in Table 1 under "Reaction with HCl." If you see no evidence of a chemical change, write *no*.

⚠ **CAUTION: Be very careful when working with acid. If you spill any acid, rinse with plenty of water and tell your teacher immediately.**

❑ **8.** Follow your teacher's instructions about how to correctly and safely dispose of the acid and other materials. Clean the beaker and test tubes.

⚠ **CAUTION: Always be careful when washing glassware. If a piece of glassware becomes cracked or broken, tell your teacher immediately.**

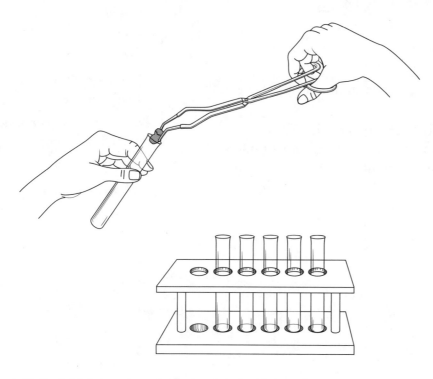

▲ **Figure 2** Testing an element's reactivity in hydrochloric acid

Name _____ Class _____ Date _____

LABORATORY CHALLENGE FOR LESSON 3-8 *(continued)*

OBSERVATIONS

Table 1: Properties of Elements			
Element	Physical Appearance	Electrical Conductivity	Reaction With HCl
Carbon			
Copper			
Iron			
Sulfur			
Aluminum			
Lead			

1. **CLASSIFY:** Which of the elements conducted electricity?

_____

2. **CLASSIFY:** Which of the elements reacted with the hydrochloric acid?

_____

3. **CLASSIFY:** Which of the elements are metals?

_____

4. **CLASSIFY:** Which elements are nonmetals?

_____

CONCLUSIONS

5. **ANALYZE:** Based on your observations in this activity, what are some general properties of metals?

_____

_____

_____

_____

6. **ANALYZE:** What are some general properties of nonmetals?

_____

_____

_____

_____

7. **INFER:** What can you infer about identifying metals and nonmetals based on physical appearance alone?

_____

_____

_____

Name _____ Class _____ Date _____

LABORATORY CHALLENGE FOR LESSON 4-6

How are ionic and covalent compounds different?

BACKGROUND: Atoms that make up compounds are held together by chemical bonds. Compounds can be either ionic or covalent, depending on the type of bonds that form among atoms in the molecule. In an ionic compound, the atoms of the combining elements gain and lose electrons, forming ions. These ions are held together by the force of attraction between oppositely charged particles. In a covalent compound, the atoms of the combining elements share electrons.

PURPOSE: In this activity, you will investigate some of the properties of ionic and covalent compounds.

PROCEDURE

❑ 1. Put on safety goggles, a lab apron, and gloves.

❑ 2. Label each of 9 pieces of paper with a name of one of the compounds.

❑ 3. Place about 1/2 teaspoon of each of the compounds on its labeled paper.

▲ **Figure 1** Place each compound on its labeled paper.

❑ 4. **OBSERVE:** Describe the physical appearance of each of the compounds. Write your observations in Table 1 on page 35.

❑ 5. Fill a beaker about one-quarter full of water.

❑ 6. **OBSERVE:** Add about 1/4 teaspoon of one of the compounds to the water in the beaker. Stir the mixture with a stirring rod for about 10 seconds and observe the mixture. If the compound dissolves in water, write *soluble* in Table 1 under "Solubility." If it does not dissolve, write *insoluble*.

Materials

safety goggles
lab apron
gloves
samples of
   baking soda
   borax
   citric acid
   cornstarch
   detergent (powdered)
   gelatin (plain)
   sugar
   table salt
pencil
9 pieces of paper
teaspoon
100-mL beaker
stirring rod
conductivity tester

❑ 7. **OBSERVE:** Place the leads of a conductivity tester into the mixture in the beaker. Observe whether or not the bulb lights. If it does, write *yes* under "Conductivity" in Table 1. If it does not, write *no*.

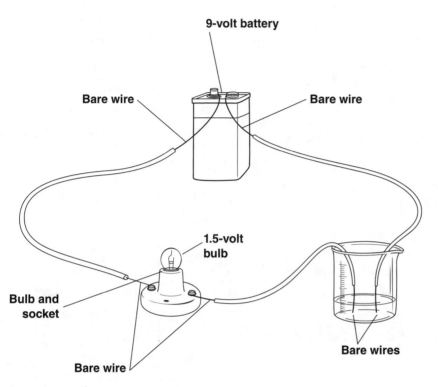

9-volt battery

Bare wire

Bare wire

1.5-volt bulb

Bulb and socket

Bare wire

Bare wires

▲ **Figure 2** Test each compound for conductivity.

❑ 8. Rinse the beaker thoroughly with clean water and dry it. Repeat Steps 5–7 for each of the other compounds. Be sure to clean and dry the beaker after each trial.

❑ 9. Carefully follow your teacher's instructions about how to correctly and safely dispose of the chemicals and other materials.

LABORATORY CHALLENGE FOR LESSON 4-6 *(continued)*

OBSERVATIONS

Table 1: Covalent and Ionic Compounds				
Compound	Description	Solubility	Conductivity	Type of Bond
Borax				
Gelatin				
Sugar				
Salt				
Baking soda				
Citric acid				
Detergent				
Cornstarch				

1. **ANALYZE:** Some characteristics of many ionic compounds include solubility in water and the ability to conduct electricity. On the basis of these two properties, which compounds appear to have ionic bonds?

    _____

    _____

2. **CLASSIFY:** Water solutions of covalent compounds do not conduct electricity. Based on this property, which compounds that you tested would you classify as covalent compounds?

    _____

    _____

3. **CLASSIFY:** Based on your answers to questions 1 and 2, complete the last column in the table by writing the type of bond for each compound.

CONCLUSIONS

4. CONTRAST: Explain how ionic and covalent compounds are different.

_____

_____

_____

_____

5. COMPARE: Did all of the compounds that conducted electricity show the same amount of conductivity? How can you tell?

_____

_____

_____

6. INFER: Solid table salt does not conduct electricity. Why do you think dissolving table salt in water allows the salt to conduct electricity?

_____

_____

_____

_____

Name _____ Class _____ Date _____

What factors affect how fast a substance dissolves?

BACKGROUND: A solute is a substance to be dissolved, and a solvent is the substance in which the solute is dissolved. Combining a solute and a solvent makes a solution. When a solute dissolves in a solvent, many factors affect the rate at which the solute dissolves.

PURPOSE: In this activity, you will investigate some of the factors that affect how fast sugar (a solute) dissolves in water (a solvent).

PROCEDURE

Part A: Effect of Temperature on Dissolving Rate

☐ **1.** Put on safety goggles and a lab apron.

☐ **2.** Using a wax pencil, label one 250-mL beaker *Cold,* a second beaker *Room temperature,* and a third beaker *Hot.*

☐ **3.** Pour 100 mL of ice-cold water into the beaker labeled "Cold."

☐ **4.** **MEASURE:** Use a thermometer to measure the temperature of the water. Record the temperature in Table 1 on page 38.

☐ **5.** **MEASURE:** Pour water at room temperature into the beaker labeled "Room temperature." Repeat Step 4.

☐ **6.** **MEASURE:** Pour hot water into the beaker labeled "Hot." Repeat Step 4.

☐ **7.** Place a sugar cube in each of the beakers. Work with one or two partners to stir the water in each beaker for 15 seconds, as shown in Figure 1.

Materials

safety goggles

lab apron

ice-cold water

250-mL beakers (3)

wax pencil

3 thermometers

room-temperature water

hot water

7 sugar cubes

stirring rod

watch or clock with second hand

mortar and pestle

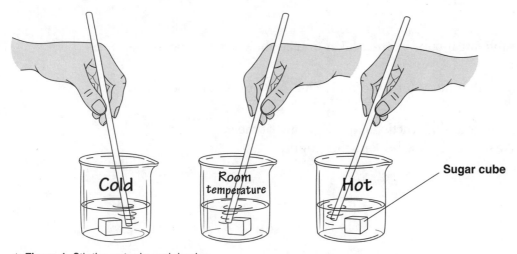

▲ **Figure 1** Stir the water in each beaker.

❑ **8. OBSERVE:** Which sugar cube dissolves fastest? Slowest? Record your observations in Table 1.

❑ **9.** Follow your teacher's instructions for disposing of the sugar-water solutions. Wash and dry the beakers thoroughly before proceeding.

Part B: Effect of Stirring on Dissolving Rate

❑ **1.** Put 100 mL of cold water into each of two 250-mL beakers.

❑ **2.** Place a sugar cube in each beaker.

❑ **3. OBSERVE:** Stir the water in one of the beakers for 30 seconds. Leave the other beaker undisturbed. Record your observations in Table 1.

❑ **4.** Follow your teacher's instructions for disposing of the sugar-water solutions. Wash and dry the beakers thoroughly before proceeding.

Part C: Effect of Particle Size on Dissolving Rate

❑ **1.** Put 100 mL of cold water into each of two beakers.

❑ **2.** Use the mortar and pestle to grind one sugar cube into a fine powder, as shown in Figure 2.

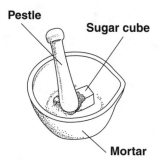

▲ **Figure 2** Grind a sugar cube with a mortar and pestle.

❑ **3.** Put the ground sugar cube in one beaker and a whole sugar cube in the other beaker.

❑ **4. OBSERVE:** Stir both beakers for 15 seconds. Record your observations in Table 1.

❑ **5.** Follow your teacher's instructions for disposing of the sugar-water solutions. Wash and dry the beakers thoroughly.

Name _____ Class _____ Date _____

LABORATORY CHALLENGE FOR LESSON 5-4 *(continued)*

OBSERVATIONS

Table 1: Rates of Dissolving in Water			
Solute	Variable	Temp.	Observations
Part A sugar	cold water		
	room-temp. water		
	hot water		
Part B sugar	stirring		
	not stirring		
Part C sugar	ground		
	not ground		

1. What variables were tested in this experiment?

   _____

   _____

   _____

2. **COMPARE:** In which situations did the sugar dissolve more rapidly?

   _____

   _____

   _____

   _____

CONCLUSIONS

3. **NAME:** Name three factors that affect how fast a solute dissolves in a solvent.

_____

_____

_____

_____

4. **INFER:** Would you expect salt to dissolve more rapidly in hot water or in cold water? Why?

_____

_____

_____

_____

5. **INFER:** Would you expect a teaspoon of sugar grains to dissolve more rapidly than a sugar cube? Why?

_____

_____

_____

_____

CRITICAL THINKING

6. **APPLY:** When mixing a lemonade mix with water, what could you do to make the lemonade mix dissolve faster and more completely?

_____

_____

_____

Name _____ Class _____ Date _____

LABORATORY CHALLENGE FOR LESSON 6-2

How do solutions, suspensions, and colloids compare?

BACKGROUND: Solutions and suspensions are different kinds of mixtures. A solution is the "best mixed" of all mixtures. A liquid solution is clear in appearance and cannot be separated by filtering. A suspension is not clear and will absorb or scatter a beam of light. A colloid suspension will scatter a beam of light. This scattering of light is called the Tyndall effect. Solutions do not show the Tyndall effect. The particles in a suspension stay mixed because of movement of the molecules of the solvent. If a suspension is left standing, it will eventually separate. Unlike a solution, a suspension can be separated by filtering. The particles in a colloid, however, are smaller than the particles in an ordinary suspension. Therefore, a colloid cannot be separated by filtering.

PURPOSE: In this activity, you will investigate some of the properties of solutions, suspensions, and colloids.

PROCEDURE

❑ 1. Put on safety goggles, a lab apron, and gloves.

❑ 2. Fill a 100-mL beaker about half full with water.

❑ 3. Use a spatula to add an amount of copper chloride ($CuCl_2$) about equal to the size of a pea to the water in the beaker.

❑ 4. Stir the mixture for about 30 sec. Then, let the contents of the beaker sit for about 1 min.

❑ 5. **OBSERVE:** Observe the mixture carefully. Is it clear or cloudy? Is undissolved material present? Record your observations in Table 1 on page 43.

❑ 6. **OBSERVE:** Use a flashlight to shine a beam of light through the beaker. Observe whether the beam is scattered or passes invisibly through the mixture. If the light beam scatters, write *yes* under "Tyndall Effect" in Table 1. If the beam does not scatter, write *no*.

Materials

safety goggles

lab apron

gloves

100-mL beakers (2)

water

spatula

copper chloride ($CuCl_2$)

stirring rod

watch or clock with
    second hand

flashlight

filter paper

plastic funnel

ring stand

metal ring

calcium carbonate
    ($CaCO_3$)

copper sulfate ($CuSO_4$)

potassium dichromate
    ($K_2Cr_2O_7$)

iron oxide (FeO)

sodium chloride ($NaCl$)

❑ 7. Fold a piece of filter paper and place it in the funnel as shown in Figure 1.

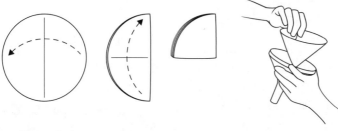

▲ **Figure 1** How to fold filter paper

❑ 8. Set up the funnel, ring stand, and an empty beaker as shown in Figure 2.

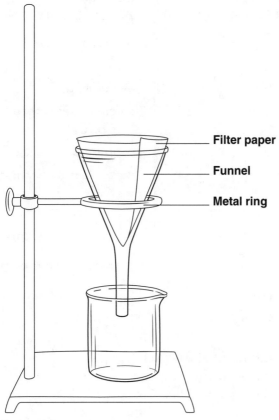

Filter paper

Funnel

Metal ring

▲ **Figure 2** Setup for filtering

❑ 9. **OBSERVE:** Filter the contents of the copper chloride mixture by slowly pouring it into the funnel. Be sure that the liquid that runs through the funnel empties into the bottom beaker. Does the mixture separate when filtered? Write *yes* or *no* in Table 1.

❑ 10. Follow your teacher's instructions for disposing of the solid and liquid materials. Thoroughly rinse out the beakers.

❑ 11. Repeat Steps 1–10 for the other chemicals listed in Table 1.

LABORATORY CHALLENGE FOR LESSON 6-2 *(continued)*

OBSERVATIONS

				Separates	Solution,
Solute	Clear or Cloudy?	Undissolved Material?	Tyndall Effect?	When Filtered?	Suspension, or Colloid?
$CuCl_2$					
$CaCO_3$					
$CuSO_4$					
$K_2Cr_2O_7$					
FeO					
$NaCl$					

Table 1: Solutions, Suspensions, and Colloids

1. **OBSERVE:** Which mixtures had a clear appearance?

_____

_____

2. **OBSERVE:** Which mixtures contained undissolved material?

_____

_____

3. **OBSERVE:** Which mixtures appeared to separate when filtered?

_____

4. **OBSERVE:** Which mixtures show the Tyndall effect?

_____

CONCLUSIONS

5. **INFER:** What are four properties of a solution?

_____

_____

_____

_____

6. **INFER:** What are four properties of a suspension?

_____

_____

_____

_____

7. **CLASSIFY:** Based on your observations, decide which of the mixtures you tested are solutions, which are suspensions, or which are both suspensions and colloids. Write your conclusions in the last column of Table 1.

CRITICAL THINKING

8. **APPLY:** Name several substances that form solutions when mixed with water.

_____

_____

_____

9. **APPLY:** Name several substances that form suspensions when mixed with water.

_____

_____

_____

LABORATORY CHALLENGE FOR LESSON 7-2

What factors can cause iron to undergo a chemical change?

BACKGROUND: A solid iron bar can be changed to a pile of iron fillings, but the change is only physical. The substance iron is not changed. However, under certain conditions, iron can be changed chemically. For example, when iron interacts with oxygen, both elements are changed chemically. A new substance called rust, or iron oxide, can be formed.

PURPOSE: In this activity, you will observe how iron changes chemically to form rust.

PROCEDURE

☐ 1. Put on safety goggles and a lab apron. Use small pieces of masking tape and a pencil to label the test tubes *A*, *B*, and *C*. Place the test tubes in a test-tube rack.

☐ 2. Use pieces of masking tape and a pencil to label two 100-mL beakers *Water* and *Oil*, as shown in Figure 1.

▲ **Figure 1** Label the 100-mL beakers.

☐ 3. **MEASURE:** Pour 50 mL of water into the beaker labeled *Water*.

☐ 4. **MEASURE:** Pour 50 mL of vegetable oil into the beaker labeled *Oil*.

☐ 5. Form three loose wads of steel wool about 3 cm in diameter. Place one piece in each of the two labeled 100-mL beakers.

Materials

safety goggles
lab apron
masking tape
pencil
3 test tubes
test-tube rack
100-mL beakers (2)
vegetable oil
water
coarse steel wool
rubber stopper
forceps
250-mL beaker
metal ring
ring stand

❑ 6. Place the third wad of steel wool into test tube A. Use a pencil to gently push the steel wool to the bottom of the tube, as shown in Figure 2. ⚠ **CAUTION: Be careful not to break the test tube.** Stopper the test tube and place it in the test-tube rack.

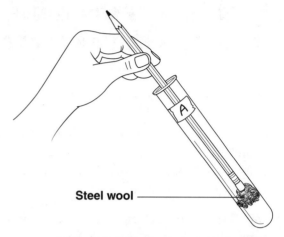

Steel wool ——————

▲ **Figure 2** Push the steel wool to the bottom of the test tube.

❑ 7. Use forceps to remove the steel wool from the oil. Place the steel wool into the bottom of test tube B. Place the test tube in the test-tube rack.

❑ 8. Using forceps, place the steel wool from the water into test tube C.

❑ 9. **MEASURE:** Add 100 mL of water to a 250-mL beaker.

❑10. Place the beaker of water on the base of a ring stand.

❑11. Use masking tape to tape the three test tubes together.

❑12. Invert the test tubes and place them in the water in the 250-mL beaker. Support the test tubes with the ring stand and metal ring, as shown in Figure 3.

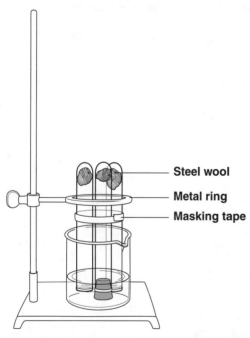

Steel wool

Metal ring

Masking tape

▲ **Figure 3** Invert the test tubes in the beaker of water.

❑13. Follow your teacher's instructions for cleanup and disposal of waste materials.

❑14. **OBSERVE:** Observe the three test tubes for 4 days. Each day, record your observations in Table 1 on page 47.

Name _____ Class _____ Date _____

LABORATORY CHALLENGE FOR LESSON 7-2 *(continued)*

OBSERVATIONS

Table 1: Rust Formation				
Test Tube	Day 1	Day 2	Day 3	Day 4
A (with stopper)				
B (with oil)				
C (with water)				

1. In which test tube did you observe a chemical change in the iron?

   _____

2. What was the purpose of test tube A?

   _____

   _____

CONCLUSIONS

3. **INFER:** Why did iron not change in all of the test tubes?

   _____

   _____

   _____

   _____

4. **CALCULATE:** The sum of the oxidation numbers for all elements in a compound must be zero. In the case of iron oxide, the total oxidation number for oxygen must cancel out the total oxidation number for iron. If the oxidation number for one atom of oxygen is –2, what is the total oxidation number for oxygen in one molecule of rust?

_____

5. **CALCULATE:** Using the answer from question 4, calculate the oxidation number for each atom of iron in the compound ferric oxide (Fe_2O_3). Explain your answer.

_____

_____

_____

_____

Name _____ Class _____ Date _____

LABORATORY CHALLENGE FOR LESSON 8-2

What is the law of conservation of matter?

Materials

safety goggles

lab apron

triple-beam balance

steel wool

tongs

Bunsen burner

250-mL beaker

water

antacid tablet

test tubes (2)

teaspoon

calcium chloride ($CaCl_2$)

sodium carbonate
  (Na_2CO_3)

stirring rod

vinegar

sodium bicarbonate
  ($NaHCO_3$)

balloon

BACKGROUND: The law of conservation of matter states that matter cannot be created or destroyed by a chemical change. This means that whenever a chemical reaction takes place, the mass of the products must be equal to the mass of the reactants. This law holds true even though the products of a chemical reaction are different from the reactants.

PURPOSE: In this activity, you will observe chemical reactions. Then you will analyze the results in terms of the law of conservation of matter.

PROCEDURE

Part A: Iron and Oxygen

❏ **1.** Put on safety goggles and a lab apron.

❏ **2.** **MEASURE:** Use a triple-beam balance to measure the mass of a piece of steel wool about 2–3 cm in diameter. Record this measurement in Table 1 on page 51.

❏ **3.** **OBSERVE:** Watch what happens as your teacher uses tongs to hold the steel wool in the flame of a Bunsen burner and heats the steel wool gently for 4 to 5 min.

❏ **4.** Allow the steel wool to cool for a few minutes. Then, use the balance to find the mass of the steel wool. Record the mass in Table 1.

❏ **5.** **CALCULATE:** Calculate the difference in the mass of the steel wool before and after being heated. Record this change in Table 1.

❏ **6.** Follow your teacher's instructions for cleanup and disposal of waste materials.

Part B: Antacid and Water

❏ **1.** Pour about 75 mL of water into a 250-mL beaker.

❏ **2.** **MEASURE:** Place the beaker with water on the balance. Then, place an antacid tablet on the balance platform next to the beaker. Find the mass of the beaker with water and the antacid tablet. Record this measurement in Table 2 on page 51.

❏ **3.** **OBSERVE:** Carefully put the antacid tablet in the water. Avoid splashing. Watch to see when the chemical reaction is complete.

❏ **4.** **MEASURE:** After the reaction is complete, find the mass of the beaker and its contents. Record your measurement in Table 2.

- ❑ 5. **CALCULATE:** Calculate the difference in mass between Steps 2 and 4. Record the change in Table 2.

- ❑ 6. Follow your teacher's instructions for cleanup and disposal of waste materials.

Part C: Sodium Carbonate and Calcium Chloride

- ❑ 1. Fill two test tubes about two-thirds full of water.

- ❑ 2. In one test tube, put about 1/2 teaspoon of calcium chloride. Use a stirring rod to mix. Then, clean the stirring rod thoroughly.

- ❑ 3. In the second test tube, put 1/2 teaspoon of sodium carbonate. Use a stirring rod to mix the chemicals.

    ⚠ **CAUTION: Be careful not to break the test tubes.**

- ❑ 4. **MEASURE:** Carefully place the two test tubes in a 250-mL beaker and find the mass of the beaker and test tubes. Record this mass in Table 3 on page 51.

- ❑ 5. Pour the contents of the two test tubes into the beaker.

- ❑ 6. **MEASURE:** Find the mass of the beaker and contents along with the two empty test tubes. Record your measurement in Table 3.

- ❑ 7. **CALCULATE:** Calculate the change in mass. Record the change in Table 3.

- ❑ 8. Follow your teacher's instructions for cleanup and disposal of waste materials.

Part D: Vinegar and Sodium Bicarbonate

- ❑ 1. Half fill a test tube with vinegar.

- ❑ 2. Put about 1/2 teaspoon of sodium bicarbonate in a balloon. Hold the balloon up by its neck so that the solid moves to the other end of the balloon, as shown in Figure 1.

- ❑ 3. Slide the neck of the balloon over the end of the test tube, being careful not to spill the sodium bicarbonate into the vinegar.

- ❑ 4. **MEASURE:** Put the balloon and test tube in a beaker and use the balance to find the mass of the beaker, balloon, and test tube. Record this measurement in Table 4 on page 51.

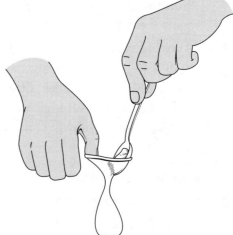

▲ **Figure 1** Place sodium bicarbonate in the balloon.

LABORATORY CHALLENGE FOR LESSON 8-2 *(continued)*

❏ **5.** Raise the end of the balloon and shake the sodium bicarbonate into the vinegar, as shown in Figure 2.

❏ **6.** **OBSERVE:** Watch for the completion of the chemical reaction.

❏ **7.** When the reaction is complete, find the mass of the beaker, balloon, and test tube. Record your measurement in Table 4.

❏ **8.** Follow your teacher's instructions for cleanup and disposal of waste materials.

❏ **9.** Wash your hands thoroughly.

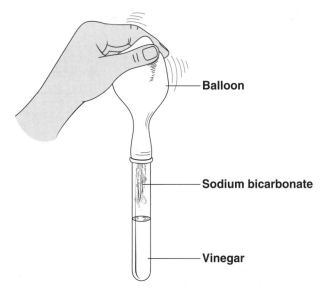

Balloon

Sodium bicarbonate

Vinegar

▲ **Figure 2** Shake the sodium bicarbonate into the vinegar.

OBSERVATIONS

Table 1: Iron and Oxygen	
Condition	**Mass**
Iron before heating	
Iron after heating	
Change in mass	

Table 2: Antacid and Water	
Condition	**Mass**
Before chemical reaction	
After chemical reaction	
Change in mass	

Table 3: Sodium Carbonate and Calcium Chloride	
Condition	**Mass**
Before chemical reaction	
After chemical reaction	
Change in mass	

Table 4: Vinegar and Sodium Bicarbonate	
Condition	**Mass**
Before chemical reaction	
After chemical reaction	
Change in mass	

1. How did the mass of the iron before heating compare with the mass of the iron after heating?

_____

_____

2. How did the masses before and after the reaction compare in Parts B, C, and D of the experiment?

_____

_____

CONCLUSIONS

3. What is the law of conservation of matter?

_____

_____

4. ANALYZE: How can you explain the difference in masses between the reactants and products in Part A? Can you think of a "hidden" reactant in this chemical reaction?

_____

_____

5. ANALYZE: How can you explain the difference in mass between the reactants and products in Part B? Can you think of an "invisible" product in the reaction?

_____

_____

_____

6. ANALYZE: How do Parts C and D demonstrate the law of conservation of matter?

_____

_____

CRITICAL THINKING

7. ANALYZE: Why is it difficult to prove the law of conservation of matter when a fuel is burned?

_____

_____

Name _____ Class _____ Date _____

LABORATORY CHALLENGE FOR LESSON 9-6

Do all solutions conduct electricity?

Materials

safety goggles

lab apron

conductivity tester

distilled water

250-mL beakers (4)

sodium chloride (NaCl)

paper towels

teaspoon

stirring rod

white sugar ($C_{12}H_{22}O_{11}$)

BACKGROUND: Distilled water contains very few ions and is, therefore, a poor conductor of electricity. In solid form, sugar and salt are also poor conductors. However, what happens when salt or sugar is dissolved in water? Do water solutions of these substances conduct electricity? Any substance that forms ions when dissolved in water is called an electrolyte. Ions are electrically charged particles that can conduct an electric current through a solution. Therefore, a water solution of an electrolyte will conduct electricity.

PURPOSE: In this activity, you will investigate the electrical conductivity of distilled water, solid sodium chloride (salt), white sugar (sucrose), and water solutions of sodium chloride and of sucrose.

PROCEDURE

❏ 1. Put on safety goggles and a lab apron.

❏ 2. Follow your teacher's instructions for setting up the conductivity tester.

❏ 3. Pour 100 mL of distilled water into a clean 250-mL beaker. Place the probes from the conductivity tester into the water in the beaker, as shown in Figure 1. ⚠ CAUTION: Be sure that the probes do not touch each other.

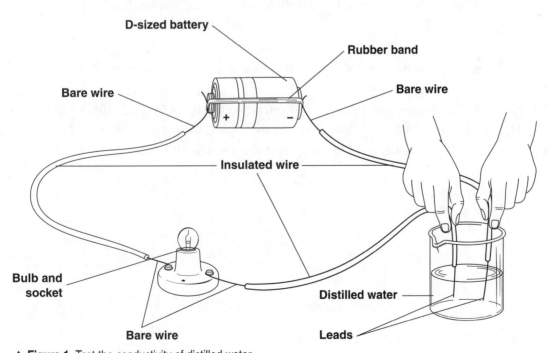

▲ **Figure 1** Test the conductivity of distilled water.

❏ **4. OBSERVE:** Observe what happens to the lightbulb. Record your observations under "Conductivity" in Table 1 on page 55. If the bulb lights, write *yes*. If the bulb does not light, write *no*.

❏ **5.** Pour sodium chloride into a clean, dry beaker until the beaker is about one-third full.

❏ **6.** Dry the probes of the conductivity tester. Place the dry probes into the sodium chloride, as shown in Figure 2.

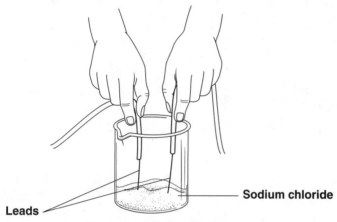

Leads   **Sodium chloride**

▲ **Figure 2** Test the conductivity of sodium chloride.

❏ **7. OBSERVE:** Observe what happens to the lightbulb. Record your observations in Table 1.

❏ **8.** Add 1 teaspoon of sodium chloride to the distilled water in the beaker. Use a stirring rod to stir the mixture until the sodium chloride is dissolved.

❏ **9.** Place the probes of the conductivity tester into the solution.

❏ **10. OBSERVE:** Observe what happens to the lightbulb. Record your observations in Table 1.

❏ **11.** Pour 100 mL of distilled water into a clean 250-mL beaker. Repeat Steps 5–10 using sugar in place of sodium chloride. Record your observations in Table 1.

❏ **12.** Follow your teacher's instructions for cleanup and disposal of all waste materials.

❏ **13.** Wash your hands thoroughly.

LABORATORY CHALLENGE FOR LESSON 9-6 *(continued)*

OBSERVATIONS

Table 1: Testing for Conductivity	
Substance	**Conductivity**
Distilled water	
Sodium chloride	
Sodium chloride solution	
Sucrose	
Sucrose solution	

1. Does distilled water conduct electricity? How do you know?

   _____

2. Does solid sodium chloride conduct electricity? How do you know?

   _____

3. Does solid sucrose conduct electricity? How do you know?

   _____

4. **RELATE:** How does adding sodium chloride affect the conductivity of distilled water?

   _____

   _____

   _____

5. **RELATE:** How does adding sucrose affect the conductivity of distilled water?

   _____

   _____

6. Are sodium chloride and sucrose electrolytes? How do you know?

_____

_____

_____

CONCLUSIONS

7. ANALYZE: What happens when an electrolyte is dissolved in water?

_____

_____

8. ANALYZE: What carries the electric current through a solution of an electrolyte in water?

_____

_____

Name _____ Class _____ Date _____

LABORATORY CHALLENGE FOR LESSON 10-5

How can tarnish be removed from silver?

BACKGROUND: Silver is a bright, shiny metal. When exposed to air, the surface of a silver object soon turns dull and has a dark gray or black color. The silver has reacted chemically with sulfur compounds in the air. A thin coating of silver sulfide, Ag_2S, has formed on the surface of the metal. In order to restore the silver to its original luster, this coating of tarnish must be removed.

PURPOSE: In this activity, you will compare methods for removing silver tarnish.

PROCEDURE

Part A: Silver Polish

❏ 1. Put on safety goggles, a lab apron, and gloves.

❏ 2. Use a soft cotton rag to apply a small amount of silver polish to the tarnished surface of a piece of silver, as shown in Figure 1. Rub vigorously with the rag until the polish turns dark.

❏ 3. Use a clean rag to wipe the polish from the silver. Observe any differences in the surface of the metal. Record your observations in Table 1 on page 59.

Materials
safety goggles
lab apron
gloves
cotton cloths or rags
silver polish
3 pieces of tarnished silver
water
plastic container (large enough to immerse the silver)
1000-mL beaker
measuring cup
baking soda
metal pot
hot plate
2 pot holders
sink
clock or watch with second hand
tongs

▲ **Figure 1** Wear gloves when applying silver polish.

Part B: Baking Soda

❑ 1. Place a tarnished silver object in a metal pot. Add enough water to the pot to cover the tarnished object.

❑ 2. **MEASURE:** Remove the object from the pot. Pour the water into the 1000-mL beaker. Measure the amount of water.

❑ 3. Using a measuring cup, measure out 1/2 cup of baking soda for every 500 mL of water in the beaker. Set this measuring cup of baking soda aside.

❑ 4. Pour the water from the beaker back into the pot. Place the tarnished piece of silver back into the pot.

❑ 5. Your teacher will place the pot on a hot plate to boil the water. Once the water is boiling, your teacher will use pot holders to remove the pot from the hot plate and place it carefully in a sink. ⚠ **CAUTION: Keep a safe distance away from the hot pot that your teacher is carrying.**

❑ 6. Slowly add the baking soda to the hot water. ⚠ **CAUTION: The water may foam. This is why the addition of the baking soda should always be done in a sink.**

❑ 7. Observe the silver object for 5 min. At the end of 5 min, use tongs to carefully remove the object from the pot.

❑ 8. Dry the object with a cloth. Observe the object and record any changes in the object in Table 1.

Part C: Baking Soda and Aluminum

❑ 1. Empty the water from the pot and line the bottom of the pot with aluminum foil.

❑ 2. Repeat Steps 1–8 in Part B with a different tarnished object.

❑ 3. Follow your teacher's instructions for cleanup and disposal of waste materials.

❑ 4. Wash your hands thoroughly.

LABORATORY CHALLENGE FOR LESSON 10-5 *(continued)*

OBSERVATIONS

Table 1: Tarnish Observations	
Methods of Tarnish Removal	**Observations**
Part A: Polish	
Part B: Baking Soda	
Part C: Baking soda and aluminum	

1. Which methods removed the silver tarnish?

   _____

   _____

   _____

2. Which method did not remove the silver tarnish?

   _____

   _____

   _____

CONCLUSIONS

3. **EXPLAIN:** What happened when the silver polish was applied to the tarnished silver?

_____

_____

4. **INFER:** What can you infer about the results obtained in Parts B and C?

_____

_____

_____

5. Describe what happened to the aluminum foil in Part C.

_____

_____

_____

6. **INFER:** What two metals reacted with the baking soda in Part C?

_____

LABORATORY CHALLENGE FOR LESSON 11-4

What happens in a nuclear chain reaction such as fission?

> **Materials**
>
> 4 sheets of construction paper
> marking pens
> 10 dominoes

BACKGROUND: On the periodic table, notice that all elements with an atomic number over 82 can undergo nuclear fission. Most fission reactions produce two or three extra neutrons. These neutrons strike other nuclei, causing more fission reactions. The process continues, producing billions of fission reactions per second. This rapid series of fission reactions is called a chain reaction.

PURPOSE: In this activity, you will demonstrate the process of nuclear fission in two different ways.

PROCEDURE

Part A: Demonstrating a Fission Reaction

❑ 1. Use marking pens to label five sheets of construction paper as follows: *Free Neutron,* two *Neutron* sheets, *Barium (Ba),* and *Krypton (Kr).*

❑ 2. Choose one classmate to act as a free neutron. This person holds the sheet of construction paper labeled *Free Neutron.*

❑ 3. All other classmates form groups of four spread out about 3 m from one another. Each of the groups represents a radioactive nucleus of uranium-235 before fission takes place.

❑ 4. Two people in each group hold the sheets of construction paper labeled *Neutron.* Another person in the group holds the sheet of paper labeled *Barium.* A fourth person in the group holds the paper labeled *Krypton.*

❑ 5. **MODEL:** When your teacher tells you to begin, the free neutron will "collide" with one of the intact nuclei of uranium-235 and begin the chain reaction. This freed neutron always moves in a straight line. ⚠ **CAUTION: Just move to the group. Do not actually collide with anyone.**

❑ 6. **MODEL:** The nucleus fissions into the elements barium and krypton. The *Barium* and the *Krypton* students should move aside to represent this action.

❏ **7. MODEL:** Two neutrons, represented by the *Neutron* students should move out in straight lines and collide with separate radioactive uranium-235 nuclei. These actions represent nuclear fission, as shown in Figure 1.

❏ **8. OBSERVE:** Observe as the chain reaction continues. Continue the colliding and splitting until all U-235 nuclei undergo fission.

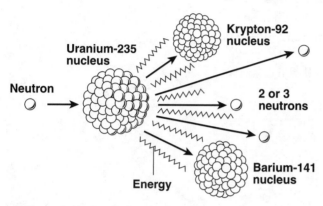

▲ **Figure 1** Nuclear fission

Part B: Demonstrating the Domino Effect

❏ **1.** Stand one domino on its end on a flat surface. Behind this domino, stand two more on their ends side-by-side so that they will fall when the first domino is pushed into them, as shown in Figure 2. Stand three dominoes on their ends side-by-side in the third row. Stand four dominoes on their ends side-by-side in the fourth row.

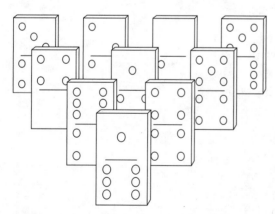

▲ **Figure 2** You can use dominoes to demonstrate a chain reaction.

❏ **2. OBSERVE:** Push the first domino into the two dominoes behind it. Observe the chain reaction.

LABORATORY CHALLENGE FOR LESSON 11-4 *(continued)*

OBSERVATIONS

1. In Part A, how many neutrons were released from each intact nucleus?

   _____

2. **COMPARE:** How were the observations in Parts A and B the same?

   _____

   _____

3. **CONTRAST:** How were the observations in Parts A and B different?

   _____

   _____

4. **INFER:** What does the domino in the first row represent?

   _____

CONCLUSIONS

5. **COMPARE:** How is the reaction in Part A similar to a nuclear chain reaction?

   _____

   _____

   _____

   _____

6. **COMPARE:** In Part B, how is the collision of a free neutron with a nucleus similar
   to fission? How is it different?

   _____

   _____

   _____

   _____

7. **INFER:** What do the dominoes in rows two through four represent?

_____

_____

_____

CRITICAL THINKING

8. **PREDICT:** Using what you know about fission reactions, how would you stop the chain reactions that you observed in both parts of this activity?

_____

_____

_____

Name _____ Class _____ Date _____

How does depth affect water pressure?

BACKGROUND: Pressure is the amount of force applied to a given area. The pressure of a fluid can be measured with a device called a manometer. A manometer is a U-shaped tube filled with a liquid, usually water. The U-tube is mounted on a board to allow the height of the liquid in either side of the U-tube to be measured. When both ends of the U-tube are open to the air, the height of liquid in both sides of the tube is the same. When one end of the tube is immersed in a fluid, however, the force of the fluid will press against the liquid and cause the height of liquid to be higher in one side of the tube than the other. When testing water, the greater the difference in the heights of the liquid in the manometer, the greater the pressure.

PURPOSE: In this activity, you will use a U-tube manometer to find out how the pressure of water changes with depth.

PROCEDURE

❑ 1. Put on safety goggles and a lab apron.

❑ 2. Stretch the open end of the rubber balloon taut over the wide end of a thistle tube. Secure it with a rubber band.

❑ 3. Attach the thistle tube lengthwise to a meter stick with two rubber bands. Be sure that the end of the thistle tube is even with the zero end of the meter stick, as shown in Figure 1.

❑ 4. Tape a manometer containing colored water to a piece of cardboard, as shown in Figure 2. Label the left side of the tube *A* and the right side *B*.

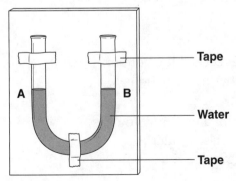

▲ **Figure 2** Attach the manometer to the cardboard.

Materials
safety goggles
lab apron
rubber balloon
thistle tube
2 rubber bands
tape
cardboard
rubber tubing
U-tube manometer, half filled with colored water
meter stick
waterproof marker
metric ruler
5-gallon plastic pail
colored water

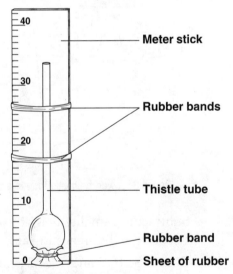

▲ **Figure 1** Attach the thistle tube to the meter stick.

❏ **5.** Attach one end of the rubber tubing to the thistle tube and the other end to the left side of the U-tube manometer.

❏ **6.** **MEASURE:** Set the manometer upright on a level surface and hold it steady. Measure the height of the liquid in side A and side B of the U-tube of the manometer. Record your measurements in Table 1 on page 67 for the depth of 0 cm. Record the difference between the height of the liquid in side A and side B for the depth of 0 cm.

❏ **7.** Use the waterproof marker to make lines on the meter stick at the following intervals: 12 cm, 24 cm, and 36 cm.

❏ **8.** **MEASURE:** Lower the thistle tube to a depth of 12 cm in the pail of water, as shown in Figure 3. Measure the height of the liquid in each side of the U-tube and record your measurements in Table 1.

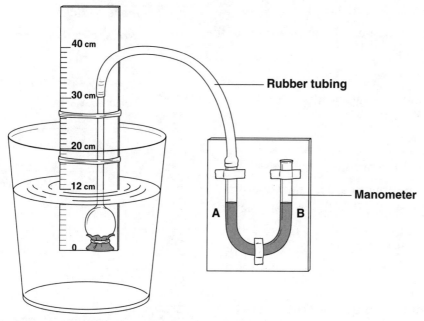

▲ **Figure 3** Lower the thistle tube to a depth of 12 cm.

❏ **9.** Subtract the smaller height from the larger height to find the difference. Record the difference in Table 1.

❏ **10.** Repeat Steps 8 and 9 for 24 cm and 36 cm.

❏ **11.** **MEASURE:** Continue these measurements until you have reached the bottom of the pail with the thistle tube. Then, follow your teacher's instructions to put away the materials and clean up your work area.

❏ **12.** **GRAPH:** Using the graph paper in Figure 4 on page 47, plot a graph of your data showing water depth versus difference in pressure. Use a ruler to connect the points of your graph. Be sure to give your graph a title.

LABORATORY CHALLENGE FOR LESSON 12-9 *(continued)*

OBSERVATIONS

Table 1: Changes in Pressure			
Depth (cm)	Height Side A (mm)	Height Side B (mm)	Difference (mm)
0			
12			
24			
36			

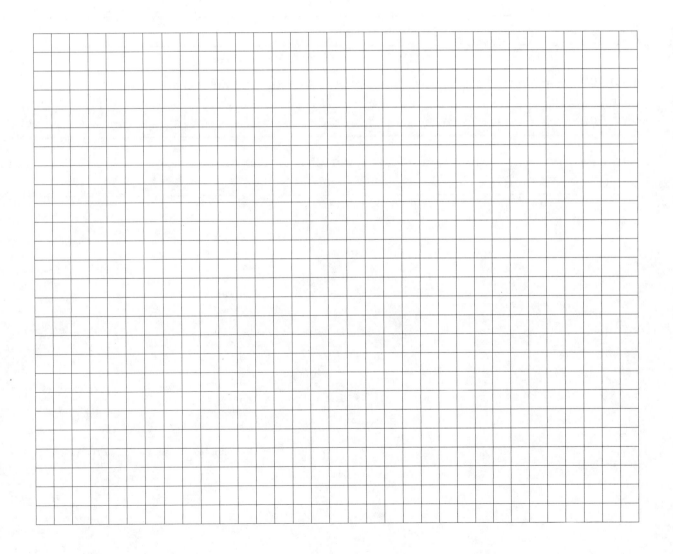

▲ **Figure 4** Graph paper

1. What is the shape of your graph?

_____

2. How does pressure change as the depth of water increases?

_____

_____

CONCLUSIONS

3. CONCLUDE: What effect does depth have on water pressure?

_____

_____

4. ANALYZE: Explain why a submarine must be built to withstand great changes in pressure.

_____

_____

_____

Name _____ Class _____ Date _____

LABORATORY CHALLENGE FOR LESSON 13-2

What happens when an object accelerates?

BACKGROUND: An object accelerates when its velocity increases or decreases or when the object changes direction. The formula for acceleration is shown below.

acceleration = change in velocity ÷ time

Because the units for velocity are distance/time, the units for acceleration become distance/time/time, or distance/(time)^2. For example, if distance is measured in meters and time in seconds, acceleration will be measured in meters/second^2.

PURPOSE: In this activity, you will learn what happens when an object accelerates.

Materials
meter stick
masking tape
1.5-m plastic ramp
ring stand
table
clamp
metric ruler
1-inch marble
stopwatch
2 different colored pencils

PROCEDURE

☐ 1. **MEASURE:** Obtain a section of pipe to be used as a ramp. Use a meter stick and masking tape to mark a starting line at 0 cm on the outside of the pipe. Make additional marks at 15 cm, 30 cm, 45 cm, 60 cm, 75 cm, 90 cm, 105 cm, 120 cm, and 135 cm.

☐ 2. Set a ring stand and clamp on the table. Tighten the clamp at a point between 6 cm and 9 cm above the tabletop. Use a metric ruler to check the height.

☐ 3. Position the ramp so that one end is resting on the clamp, as shown in Figure 1.

☐ 4. Place a marble at the top of the ramp. Have your lab partner ready with a stopwatch to time the movement of the marble as it rolls down the ramp.

☐ 5. **MEASURE:** Release the marble. Use the stopwatch to time how long it takes the marble to reach the 15-cm mark. Record the measurement in Table 1 on page 71.

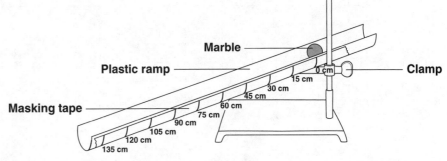

▲ **Figure 1** Rest one end of the ramp on the clamp.

❏ **6.** Repeat Steps 4 and 5 for each of the remaining distances marked on the ramp.

❏ **7.** **CALCULATE:** For each time measurement that you make, use the following formulas to calculate average velocity and final velocity.

average velocity = distance ÷ time

final velocity = 2 × average velocity

Record your answers in Table 1.

❏ **8.** **CALCULATE:** Calculate acceleration for each time measurement by using the following formula.

acceleration = final velocity ÷ time

Record your answers in Table 1.

❏ **9.** **MEASURE:** Raise the ramp to produce a steeper angle. The upper end should be between 10 and 12 cm above the tabletop. Use a metric ruler to check the height.

❏**10.** Repeat Steps 4–8 and record your results in Table 2.

❏**11.** **GRAPH:** Using the graph paper in Figure 2, make a graph of distance versus time for the data you recorded in Table 1 and Table 2. Use a different colored pencil for each line of the graph. Give your graph a title.

Concepts and Challenges in Physical Science, Laboratory Manual © Pearson Education, Inc./Globe Fearon/Pearson Learning Group. All rights reserved. Copying strictly prohibited.

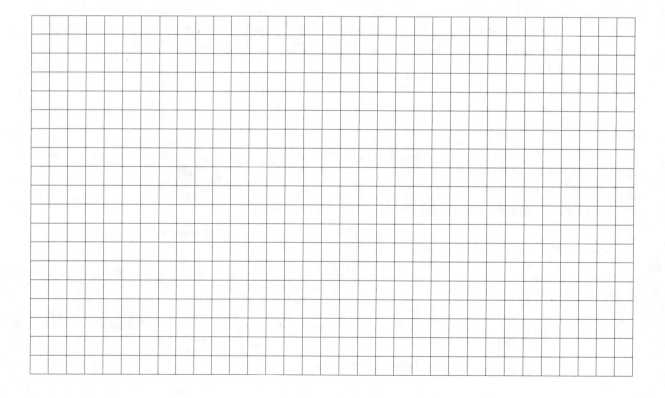

▲ **Figure 2** Graph paper

LABORATORY CHALLENGE FOR LESSON 13-2 *(continued)*

OBSERVATIONS

Table 1: Acceleration With the Low Ramp				
Distance (cm)	Time (sec)	Average Velocity (cm/sec)	Final Velocity (cm/sec)	Acceleration (cm/sec/sec)
0				
15				
30				
45				
60				
75				
90				
105				
120				
135				

Table 2: Acceleration With the Higher Ramp				
Distance (cm)	Time (sec)	Average Velocity (cm/sec)	Final Velocity (cm/sec)	Acceleration (cm/sec/sec)
0				
15				
30				
45				
60				
75				
90				
105				
120				
135				

1. Did the marble travel down the ramp at a constant velocity? How do you know?

_____

_____

_____

2. **OBSERVE:** What effect did raising the ramp have on the marble's velocity?

_____

_____

CONCLUSIONS

3. **CONCLUDE:** Did the marble accelerate? How do you know?

_____

4. **INFER:** What force caused the marble to accelerate?

_____

5. **INFER:** If you continued to raise one end of the ramp, in what position would the marble have its greatest velocity?

_____

_____

6. **INFER:** In what position of the ramp would the marble have its greatest acceleration?

_____

_____

_____

7. **HYPOTHESIZE:** What would happen if the marble was allowed to keep rolling off the ramp and onto the table? Explain your answer.

_____

_____

_____

Name _____ Class _____ Date _____

LABORATORY CHALLENGE FOR LESSON 14-5

How is work calculated?

BACKGROUND: Many people think of work as something they do to earn a living or to accomplish a task, such as homework. A scientist, however, has a much more specific idea of work. To a scientist, work is done only if three things happen:

1. A force is exerted on an object.
2. The object on which the force is exerted moves.
3. The object moves in the direction of the force.

The formula for calculating work is shown below.

Work = force × distance

Work is measured in units of force (newtons) multiplied by units of distance (meters), or newton-meters (N-m).

PURPOSE: In this activity, you will do work on an object and then calculate the amount of work you have done.

PROCEDURE

☐ **1. MEASURE:** Hang the friction block from the spring scale and read the weight of the block in newtons, as shown in Figure 1. Record your measurement in Table 1 on page 74.

☐ **2. CALCULATE:** Find the weight of a 200-g mass in newtons by using the following formula.

Weight in newtons = mass in kg × 9.8

Record the weight of a 200-g mass in newtons in Table 1.

☐ **3.** Look at Table 2 on page 75. Using the weight of the friction block and the weight of each 200-g mass, fill in the column "Weight of Block and Masses (N)" for Trial 1. Be sure to add the correct number of masses for each trial.

☐ **4.** Lay the friction block on a flat surface. Place one 200-g mass on the friction block and pass the hook of the spring scale through the screw eye of the friction block. Hold the other end of the scale in your hand.

▲ **Figure 1** Measure the weight of the friction block.

Materials

friction block
0-5 newton spring scale
200-g masses (3)
meter stick

Concepts and Challenges in Physical Science, Laboratory Manual © Pearson Education, Inc./Globe Fearon/Pearson Learning Group. All rights reserved. Copying strictly prohibited.

CHAPTER 14: Energy and Work 73

❑ **5.** Lay the meter stick next to the friction block, as shown in Figure 2. Line up the end of the block with the zero end of the meter stick.

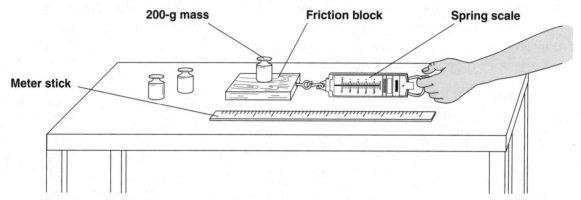

200-g mass   **Friction block**   **Spring scale**

Meter stick

▲ **Figure 2** Line up the end of the block with the end of the meter stick.

❑ **6. MEASURE:** Using a steady force, pull the block and mass a distance of 0.5 meter. As you pull, read the force in newtons on the spring scale. Record your measurement in Table 1 under "Force."

❑ **7.** Add a second 200-g mass to the block and repeat Step 6.

❑ **8.** Add a third 200-g mass to the block and repeat Step 6.

❑ **9.** Remove two of the three masses so that you once again have only one mass on the block.

❑ **10. MEASURE:** Pull the block and mass a distance of 1 m. Read the force in newtons on the spring scale as you pull. Record your measurement in Table 2.

❑ **11.** Repeat Step 10 with two masses and three masses on the friction block.

❑ **12. CALCULATE:** Calculate the work for each of the six trials, using the following formula.

> Work = force × distance

OBSERVATIONS

Table 1: Weights	
Weight of block in Step 1 (N)	
Weight of 200-g mass in Step 2 (N)	

Name _____ Class _____ Date _____

LABORATORY CHALLENGE FOR LESSON 14-5 *(continued)*

			Table 2: Doing Work		
Trial	Number of Masses	Weight of Block and Masses (N)	Force (N)	Distance (m)	Work (N-m)
1	1			0.5	
2	2			0.5	
3	3			0.5	
4	1			1.0	
5	2			1.0	
6	3			1.0	

1. **RELATE:** How did the amount of work change as the number of masses increased?

_____

_____

_____

2. **RELATE:** How did the amount of work change as the distance increased?

_____

_____

_____

CONCLUSIONS

3. How is work calculated?

_____

_____

_____

4. **ANALYZE:** Suppose you placed wheels or ball bearings under the block. How do you think this would affect the amount of work that would be required to move the block and masses? Explain your answer.

_____

_____

_____

_____

_____

Name _____ Class _____ Date _____

How can you find the efficiency of a machine?

Materials

safety goggles
friction block
5 books
1-m wooden ramp
spring scale
200-g masses (2)
masking tape
meter stick

BACKGROUND: A machine can make work easier by reducing the amount of force that you have to exert. A machine can also reduce the amount of time needed to do work. However, a machine does not reduce the *amount* of work done. Work must be put into a machine in order for work to come out of the machine. For any machine, the ratio of work output to work input is called the efficiency of the machine. Efficiency is usually expressed as a percentage. The efficiency of a machine can never be as great as 100% because some input work is always "lost" in overcoming friction.

PURPOSE: In this activity, you will use a simple machine, a ramp, to do work, and you will find the efficiency of the ramp.

PROCEDURE

☐ **1.** Put on safety goggles. Place two 200-g masses on the friction block. Tape the masses to the block.

☐ **2.** **MEASURE:** Use a spring scale to find the weight of the block and masses in newtons. Record this weight under "Resistance (N)" in Table 1 on page 79.

☐ **3.** Use books to raise one end of the ramp to a height of about 5 cm, as shown in Figure 1. Measure and record the exact height in meters under "Resistance Distance" in Table 1.

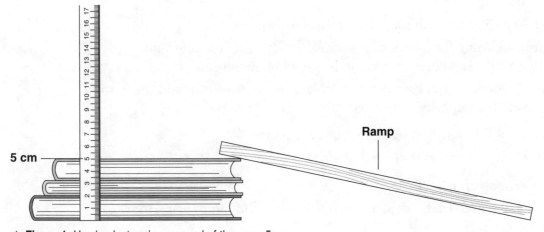

▲ **Figure 1** Use books to raise one end of the ramp 5 cm.

❏ **4. MEASURE:** Measure the length of the ramp. Record this measurement, in meters, under "Effort Distance (m)" in Table 1. This value will be the same for each trial, so fill the entire column now.

❏ **5.** Place the friction block and masses on the ramp. Attach the spring scale to the block, as shown in Figure 2.

❏ **6.** Applying a steady force, use the spring scale to pull the friction block and masses up the ramp. While pulling, read the spring scale. Record this value under "Effort (N)" in Table 1.

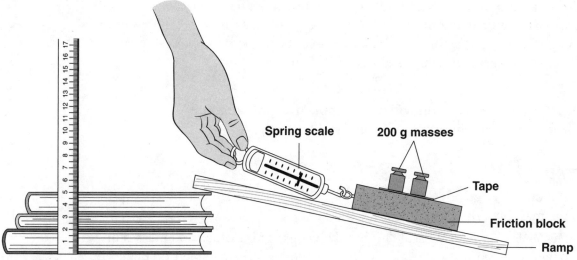

▲ **Figure 2** Attach the spring scale to the friction block.

❏ **7.** Use additional books to raise the height of the ramp to about 10 cm. Measure and record the exact height in meters under "Resistance Distance (m)" in Table 1.

❏ **8.** Repeat Steps 5 and 6 with the ramp at this height.

❏ **9.** Continue adjusting the height of the ramp, about 5 cm at a time, and repeating Steps 5 and 6, up to a ramp height of about 40 cm.

❏**10. CALCULATE:** For each trial completed, calculate the work output and the work input, using the following formulas.

> Work output = resistance × resistance distance
>
> Work input = effort × effort distance

Record your answers in Table 1.

❏**11. CALCULATE:** For each trial, calculate the efficiency of the ramp, using the following formula.

$$\text{Efficiency} = \frac{\text{W out}}{\text{W in}} \times 100$$

Record the efficiency for each trial in Table 1. (Hint: This is always a percent.)

Name _____ Class _____ Date _____

LABORATORY CHALLENGE FOR LESSON 15-2 *(continued)*

OBSERVATIONS

Table 1: Finding Efficiency						
Resistance Distance (m)	Effort Distance (m)	Resistance (N)	Effort (N)	Work Input (N-m)	Work Output (N-m)	Efficiency (%)

1. **RELATE:** How did the effort force change as the resistance distance changed?

_____

_____

2. **RELATE:** How did the efficiency of the machine change as the resistance distance changed?

_____

_____

CONCLUSIONS

3. **APPLY:** How can you find the efficiency of a simple machine?

_____

_____

_____

4. **INFER:** How would the efficiency of this simple machine be changed if you were to wax the ramp or place rollers under the friction block? Explain.

_____

_____

_____

LABORATORY CHALLENGE FOR LESSON 16-9

What happens to liquids when they are heated?

BACKGROUND: The kinetic-molecular theory of matter states that when matter is heated, the particles (molecules) that make up the matter move faster. As the molecules move faster, they move farther apart and occupy more space. This means that the substance expands and its volume increases.

PURPOSE: In this activity, you will observe how water expands when heated. Then, you will compare its rate of expansion with the rates for two other liquids.

PROCEDURE

1. Put on safety goggles and a lab apron.
2. Fill a beaker with water to about 2 cm from the top.
3. Place a heat source on the base of the ring stand. Place the beaker on the heat source.
4. Obtain a test tube, rubber stopper, and glass tubing apparatus from your teacher.
5. Fill the test tube with water and insert the stopper into the test tube. Make sure that when the stopper is inserted, water is forced up into the glass tubing. There should be 15–20 mm of water in the tubing, as shown in Figure 1. There should be no air bubbles between the stopper and the water in the test tube.
6. Attach the test tube apparatus to the ring stand, using the burette clamp, as shown in Figure 2. Make sure that the test tube is straight and that it does not touch the sides or bottom of the beaker.

Materials

safety goggles
lab apron
600-mL beaker
water
heat source
test tube, stopper, glass tubing apparatus
wax pencil
thermometer
ring stand
burette clamp
thermometer clamp
3 different-colored pencils
metric ruler

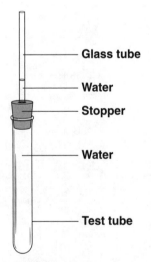

▲ **Figure 1** The stopper should force water up into the glass tubing.

Glass tube
Water
Stopper
Water
Test tube

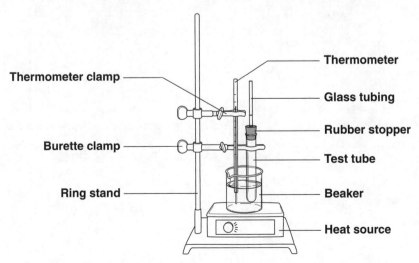

Thermometer clamp
Burette clamp
Ring stand

Thermometer
Glass tubing
Rubber stopper
Test tube
Beaker
Heat source

▲ **Figure 2** Make sure that the test tube does not touch the beaker.

❏ **7.** Use a wax pencil to mark the height of the water column in the glass tubing. This mark will be your zero mark.

❏ **8.** **OBSERVE:** Place a thermometer in the beaker. Secure it with a thermometer clamp so that the thermometer does not touch the sides or bottom of the beaker. Observe the temperature of the water. Record this temperature in Table 1 on page 83 as the "Start" temperature.

❏ **9.** Have your teacher adjust the heat source and begin heating the water.
⚠ **CAUTION: Be sure to observe safety rules for using a heat source.**

❏ **10.** As the water heats, continually watch the temperature. When the temperature reaches 30°C, measure the height of the water column above the mark you made earlier. Record this measurement in millimeters in Table 1.

❏ **11.** As the water continues to heat, repeat Step 10 for 40°C, 50°C, 60°C, 70°C, 80°C, and 90°C.

❏ **12.** **GRAPH:** In addition to the data you collected for the expansion of water, Table 1 also contains information about the expansion of glycerin and alcohol. Use the data in the table and the graph paper in Figure 3 to make a graph of expansion vs. temperature for water, glycerin, and alcohol. Use a different colored pencil for each liquid. Label each graph line for the liquid it represents.

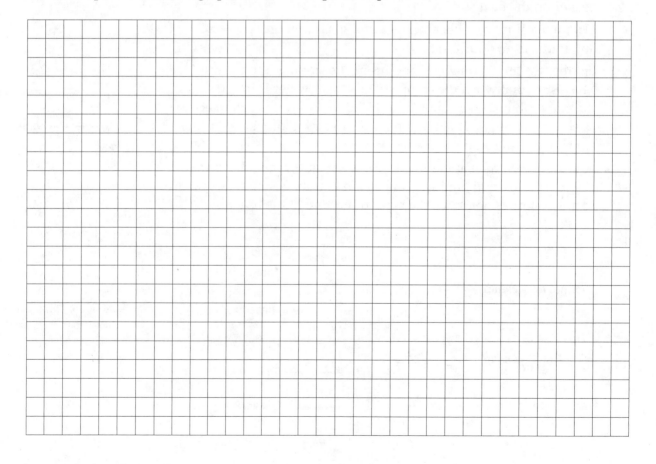

▲ **Figure 3** Graph paper

Name _____ Class _____ Date _____

LABORATORY CHALLENGE FOR LESSON 16-9 *(continued)*

OBSERVATIONS

Table 1: Expansion of Liquids			
Temperature (°C)	Height of Liquid Column (mm)		
	Water	Glycerin	Alcohol
Start:	*0*	*0*	*0*
30		*8*	*21*
40		*19*	*32*
50		*27*	*59*
60		*38*	*97*
70		*52*	*123*
80		*70*	*165*
90		*91*	*215*

1. With what other liquids is water compared in Table 1?

   _____

   _____

2. **COMPARE:** Which of the three liquids expands most when heated? Which expands least?

   _____

   _____

   _____

   _____

CONCLUSIONS

3. **INFER:** What happens to the molecules of a liquid when the liquid is heated? How does this affect the volume of the liquid?

_____

_____

_____

4. **CONCLUDE:** Do all liquids expand at the same rate? How do you know?

_____

_____

_____

Name _____ Class _____ Date _____

LABORATORY CHALLENGE FOR LESSON 17-3

What factors affect the transfer of mechanical energy by waves?

Materials

safety goggles

lab apron

water

foil pan or plastic
    container

metric ruler

adjustable, 3-speed
    electric fan

stopwatch or watch
    with second hand

large rock

BACKGROUND: Water waves can be formed by friction between the water and the moving air. When wind blows over the surface of water, energy is transferred from the wind to the water, causing waves to form. This energy is then transferred through the water in the form of waves.

PURPOSE: In this activity, you will observe two factors that determine the size of ocean waves.

PROCEDURE

Part A: Measuring Wave Height

❑ 1. Put on safety goggles and a lab apron.

❑ 2. Pour water into a foil pan to about two-thirds full. Use a metric ruler to measure the depth of the water.

❑ 3. Place an electric fan about 8 cm from one end of the pan, as shown in Figure 1. Adjust the fan so that it is angled directly toward the surface of the water. ⚠ **CAUTION: Do not let any part of the fan come into contact with the water.**

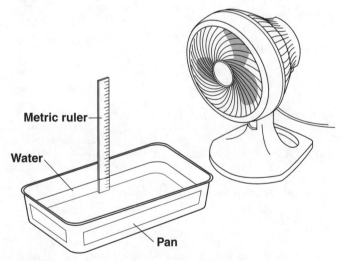

▲ **Figure 1** Place the fan near the pan of water.

❑ 4. Turn on the fan. Set its speed at the lowest setting. ⚠ **CAUTION: Do not put your fingers near the fan blades while the fan is operating.**

❑ 5. After 1 min, set the metric ruler in the pan against the inside edge to measure the height of the waves. Try to make as accurate a measurement as possible. Record your measurement in Table 1 on page 87.

❑ **6.** After 3 min, measure the height of the waves again. Make your measurement at the same point in the pan. Record your measurement in Table 1.

❑ **7.** Repeat Steps 4–6 with the fan set at the medium setting and again at the high setting. Remember to record your measurements.

Part B: Measuring Obstructed Wave Height

❑ **1.** Using the same setup as you did in Part A, place a rock in the center of the pan, as shown in Figure 2. The rock should rise above the surface of the water.

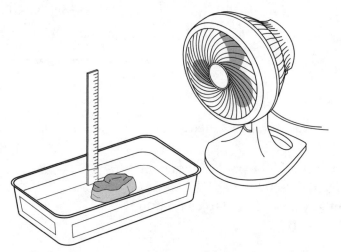

▲ **Figure 2** The rock should rise above the surface of the water.

❑ **2.** Turn the fan to the lowest setting. After 1 min, set the metric ruler against the inside edge of the pan to measure the height of the waves. Record your measurement in Table 2 on page 87.

❑ **3.** After 3 min, measure the height of the wave again. Record your measurement in Table 2.

❑ **4.** Repeat Steps 2–3 with the fan set at the highest setting. Record your measurements in Table 2.

❑ **5.** Follow your teacher's instructions for cleaning up your work area.

LABORATORY CHALLENGE FOR LESSON 17-3 (continued)

OBSERVATIONS

Table 1: Measuring Wave Height		
	Height of Wave	
Fan Setting	**After 1 Min**	**After 3 Min**
Low		
Medium		
High		

Table 2: Measuring Obstructed Wave Height		
	Height of Wave	
Fan Setting	**After 1 Min**	**After 3 Min**
Low		
High		

1. Which fan setting produced the lowest waves?

   _____

   _____

2. Which fan setting produced the highest waves?

   _____

   _____

3. How did the rock affect wave motion in Part B?

   _____

   _____

   _____

4. How were the waves different after 1 min and 3 min in Part B?

_____

_____

_____

CONCLUSIONS

5. CONCLUDE: How is wave height affected by the wind speed?

_____

_____

6. CONCLUDE: How is wave height affected by the amount of time the wind blows?

_____

_____

7. INFER: How is wave height related to the amount of energy being transferred?

_____

_____

8. INFER: How did the rock affect the transfer of energy by waves?

_____

_____

_____

9. CONCLUDE: What factors affect wave height in this activity?

_____

LABORATORY CHALLENGE FOR LESSON 18-4

How can the speed of sound through air be measured?

BACKGROUND: Sound travels at different speeds through different mediums. For example, sound waves travel much faster through solids than they do through air. The temperature of a medium also affects the speed of sound.

PURPOSE: In this activity, you will measure the speed of sound through air in two different ways.

PROCEDURE

Part A: Calculating Speed When Distance Is Known

❑ 1. **MEASURE:** In a large, open (outdoor) area, use a metric tape measure to mark off a distance of about 350 meters. Record the exact distance in Table 1 on page 91. The distance will remain the same for all four trials.

❑ 2. Stand at one end of the measured distance with a whistle and a brightly colored cloth. Have a partner stand at the other end with a stopwatch.

❑ 3. When your partner is ready, blow the whistle as loudly as you can. At the same instant, wave the brightly colored cloth in the air.

❑ 4. Have your partner start the stopwatch when he or she sees the colored cloth being waved and stop the watch when he or she hears the sound of the whistle. Record the number of seconds in Table 1.

❑ 5. Repeat Steps 3 and 4.

❑ 6. Change places with your partner. Repeat Steps 3 and 4 two more times.

❑ 7. You should have four measurements for time. Find the average of the four times and record the average in Table 1.

❑ 8. **CALCULATE:** Calculate the speed of sound for each trial, using the following formula.

Speed = distance ÷ time

Record the speed of sound for each trial in Table 1.

❑ 9. **CALCULATE:** Calculate the average speed by using the following formula.

Average speed = distance ÷ average time

Record the average speed of sound in Table 1.

Materials

safety goggles

lab apron

metric tape measure

whistle

brightly colored cloth

stopwatch

container (25 cm deep)

water

4 tuning forks of different frequencies

large rubber stopper

metal tube

utility clamp

ring stand

metric ruler

Part B: Calculating Speed When Frequency Is Known

❏ **1.** Put on safety goggles and a lab apron. Fill a 25-cm container with water and set up your apparatus, as shown in Figure 1.

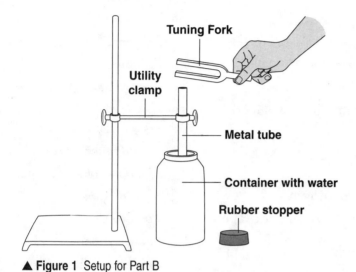

▲ **Figure 1** Setup for Part B

❏ **2.** Look at the number on the tuning fork. This number is the tuning fork's frequency. Record the frequency of the tuning fork in Table 2 on page 91.

❏ **3.** Strike the tuning fork on a rubber stopper and hold it over the metal tube.

❏ **4.** Loosen the clamp and adjust the position of the tube until the tone resonates, or sounds louder.

❏ **5.** When the tube produces maximum resonance, tighten the clamp with the tube in this position.

❏ **6.** Measure the distance from the surface of the water to the top of the tube. Record this measurement, in meters, in Table 2 under "Length of Metal Tube (m)."

❏ **7.** To find the wavelength of the sound wave, multiply the length of the metal tube by 4. Record the wavelength in Table 2.

❏ **8.** Repeat Steps 3–8 for each of the other three tuning forks.

❏ **9.** **CALCULATE:** To find the speed of the sound wave for each tuning fork, use the following formula.

Speed = frequency × wavelength

Record the speed for each tuning fork in Table 2.

❏**10.** Find the average of the four speeds. Record the average on the line provided below Table 2.

❏**11.** Follow your teacher's instructions for cleaning up your work area.

LABORATORY CHALLENGE FOR LESSON 18-4 *(continued)*

OBSERVATIONS

Table 1: Speed of Sound, Using a Whistle			
Trial	Distance (m)	Time (sec)	Speed (m/sec)
1			
2			
3			
4			
Average			

Table 2: Speed of Sound, Using a Tuning Fork				
Trial Number	Frequency of Tuning Fork	Length of Metal Tube (m)	Wavelength (m)	Speed (m/sec)
1				
2				
3				
4				

Average Speed: _____

1. How do your average values for the speed of sound compare in Tables 1 and 2? What might be some reasons for any differences?

   _____

   _____

   _____

   _____

2. How do your values for the speed of sound compare for each of the four tuning forks?

_____

_____

_____

_____

CONCLUSIONS

3. INFER: In Part A, why do you see the waving cloth before hearing the whistle?

_____

_____

4. What is the average speed of sound in air?

_____

_____

CRITICAL THINKING

5. ANALYZE: If you were to perform Part A of this experiment on a different day in a different place, would you expect to achieve exactly the same results? Explain your answer.

_____

_____

_____

6. ANALYZE: Does the frequency of a sound change its speed? Explain your answer.

_____

_____

_____

LABORATORY CHALLENGE FOR LESSON 19-6

How is light refracted?

BACKGROUND: When light passes from one substance into another, such as from air into glass, the light rays are refracted, or bent. Refraction occurs because the speed of light changes when it passes from a medium of one density into another medium of a different density.

PURPOSE: In this activity, you will observe how light is refracted by a convex lens, a concave lens, and a refraction plate. Then, you will learn how a refraction plate can be used to measure and compare the angle of incidence and the angle of emergence.

Materials

masking tape
white paper
book
comb
light source
double convex lens
pencil
double concave lens
glass refraction plate
metric ruler
protractor

PROCEDURE

Part A: Refraction Through Convex and Concave Lenses

☐ 1. Use masking tape to attach a sheet of white paper to the cover of a book.

☐ 2. Tape a comb to the spine of the book. The teeth of the comb should extend above the edge of the book, as shown in Figure 1.

☐ 3. In a darkened room, have a lab partner hold a light source about 1 m from the comb and shine a beam of light through the teeth of the comb. Observe the parallel rays of light on the paper.

☐ 4. While your partner continues to hold the light steady, place a double convex lens in the beam of light between the book and the light source, as shown in Figure 2.

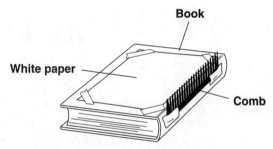

▲ **Figure 1** Attach a sheet of paper and a comb to a book.

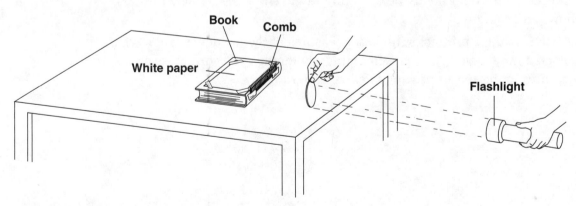

▲ **Figure 2** Shine a beam of light through a convex lens.

❏ 5. **OBSERVE:** Observe the light beam as it passes through the convex lens. Complete Diagram 1 on page 95 by sketching the rays of light as they pass through the lens and out the other side.

❏ 6. Replace the convex lens with a double concave lens and repeat Steps 4 and 5. Complete Diagram 2 on page 95 by sketching the rays of light as they pass through the lens.

Part B: Using a Glass Refraction Plate

❏ 1. Set a refraction plate on a sheet of white paper and trace around it.

❏ 2. Have your partner shine a beam of light into the side of the refraction plate. The light should be held so that the beam strikes the plate at an acute angle about 3 cm from one corner of the plate, as shown in Figure 3.

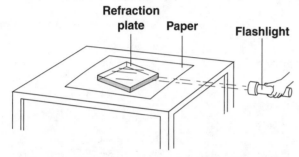

▲ **Figure 3** Shine a beam of light into a refraction plate.

❏ 3. On the paper, draw a dot to mark the point where the light leaves the light source and another dot where the incident ray strikes the refraction plate. Draw a third dot to mark the point where the ray of light emerges from the refraction plate and a fourth dot farther along the emerging ray.

❏ 4. Turn off the light source and remove the glass plate from the paper. Use a ruler to draw the incident ray and the emerging ray on the sheet of paper. Connect the incident ray to the emerging ray to show the refracted ray, as shown in Diagram 3.

❏ 5. **MEASURE:** Using a protractor, find the measures of the incidence (angle x), the refracted ray (angle y), and the emerging ray (angle e). Record these angle measures in the spaces provided next to Diagram 3.

LABORATORY CHALLENGE FOR LESSON 19-6 *(continued)*

OBSERVATIONS

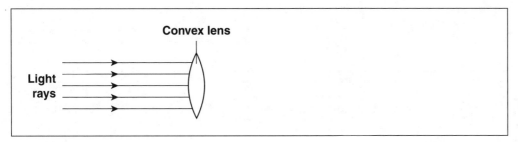

▲ Diagram 1

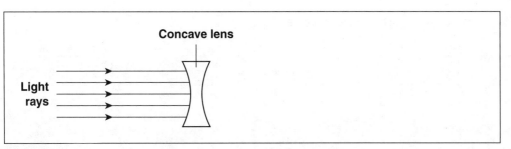

▲ Diagram 2

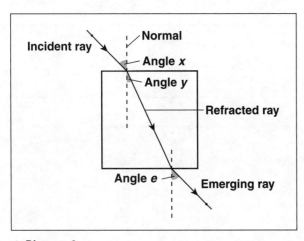

▲ Diagram 3

Angle x _____

Angle y _____

Angle e _____

1. **COMPARE:** In your diagram of the refraction plate, how does the angle of incidence (angle *x*) compare with the angle of refraction (angle *y*)?

_____

_____

2. **COMPARE:** How does the angle of incidence (angle *x*) compare with the angle of emergence (angle *e*)?

_____

_____

3. What is true about the incident ray and the emerging ray?

_____

_____

CONCLUSIONS

4. **CONCLUDE:** How does a double convex lens refract light?

_____

_____

5. **CONCLUDE:** How does a double concave lens refract light?

_____

_____

Name _____ Class _____ Date _____

LABORATORY CHALLENGE FOR LESSON 20-3

How are electrical conductors different from insulators?

BACKGROUND: Material can be classified as a conductor or an insulator, depending on whether or not electricity flows through it easily. Materials through which electrons pass easily are called conductors. Materials through which electrons do not pass easily are called insulators.

PURPOSE: In this activity, you will test different materials for their resistance or conductivity.

PROCEDURE

Part A: Resistance

☐ **1.** Put on safety goggles.

☐ **2.** **OBSERVE:** Set the ohmmeter on low. Then, test each of the materials by touching the leads to the material, as shown in Figure 1. Observe whether the resistance of each material is high (above the middle mark) or low (below the middle mark). Then, write *high* or *low* under "Resistance" in Table 1 on page 99 for each material.

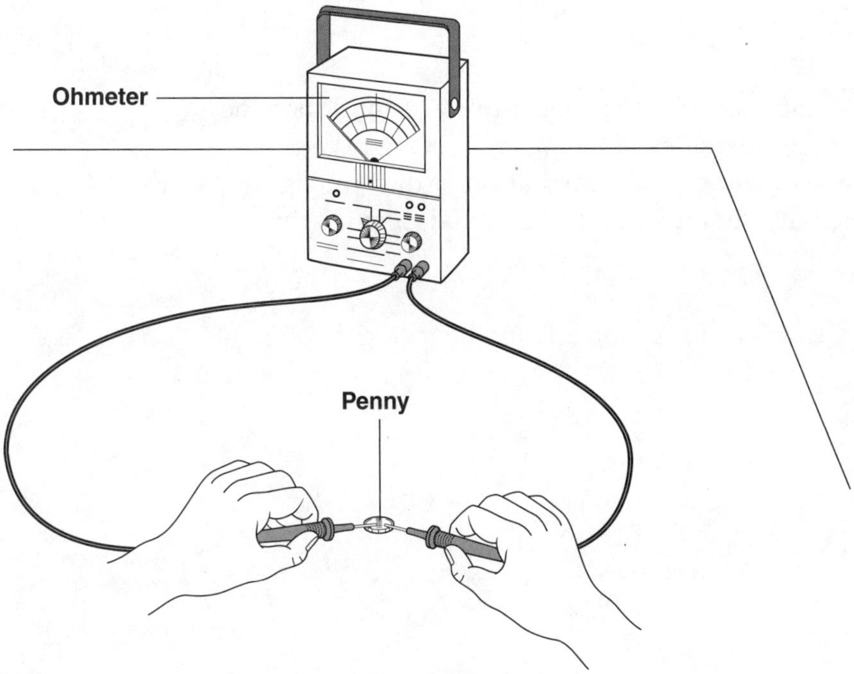

Materials

safety goggles

ohmmeter

aluminum foil
   (3 cm × 3 cm)

penny

glass

plastic cup

plastic wrap
   (3 cm × 3 cm)

paper clip

thick rubber band

conductivity tester

Ohmeter ————

Penny

▲ **Figure 1** Test the resistance of each material.

Part B: Conductors or Insulators?

❏ **1.** Set up the conductivity tester, as shown in Figure 2.

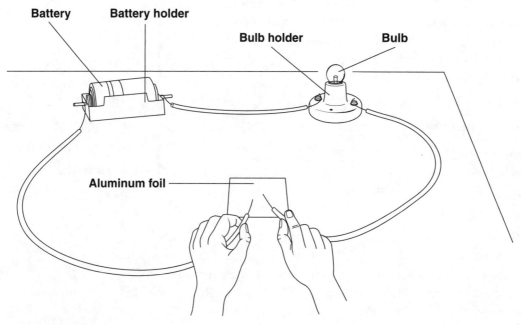

▲ **Figure 2** Conductivity tester

❏ **2.** **OBSERVE:** Test each of the materials with the conductivity tester. Touch the bare ends of the wire to opposites sides of the material being tested.
⚠ **CAUTION: Hold the two wires by the insulation.** If the bulb lights, write *yes* under "Conductivity" in the table. If the bulb does not light, write *no*.

❏ **3.** Follow your teacher's instructions for putting away the materials.

Name _____ Class _____ Date _____

LABORATORY CHALLENGE FOR LESSON 20-3 *(continued)*

OBSERVATIONS

Table 1: Resistance, Conductors, and Insulators		
Material	**Resistance**	**Conductivity**
Aluminum foil		
Penny		
Glass		
Plastic cup		
Plastic wrap		
Paper clip		
Rubber band		

1. **CLASSIFY:** Which of the materials that you tested showed high resistance? Which of the materials showed low resistance?

_____

_____

2. What kind of electric circuit is represented in Part B of this activity?

_____

3. **CLASSIFY:** Which of the materials that you tested showed high conductivity? Which of the materials showed low conductivity?

_____

_____

CONCLUSIONS

4. **DEFINE:** What is a conductor?

_____

_____

5. **DEFINE:** What is an insulator?

_____

_____

6. **ANALYZE:** What properties of matter did you test for in this activity?

_____

7. **INFER:** How is resistance related to electrical conductivity?

_____

_____

_____

Name _____ Class _____ Date _____

LABORATORY CHALLENGE FOR LESSON 21-2

What is the shape of a magnetic field?

Materials

safety goggles

2 bar magnets of equal strength

large piece of stiff, white paper

piece of clear, stiff plastic

pepper shaker filled with iron filings

small funnel

horseshoe magnet

BACKGROUND: The region surrounding a magnet in which magnetic forces act is called a magnetic field. The action of magnetic forces produce a regular pattern all around the magnet. Magnetism is stronger at certain places than at others on a magnet.

PURPOSE: In this activity, you will determine the shape of a magnetic field around two types of magnets. You will also see what happens when two magnetic fields are brought close to each other.

PROCEDURE

Part A: Magnetic Field Around Single Magnets

❑ **1.** Put on safety goggles. Place one of the bar magnets on a piece of white paper. Place a piece of clear plastic over the magnet.

❑ **2.** Carefully sprinkle iron filings on the piece of plastic, as shown in Figure 1.

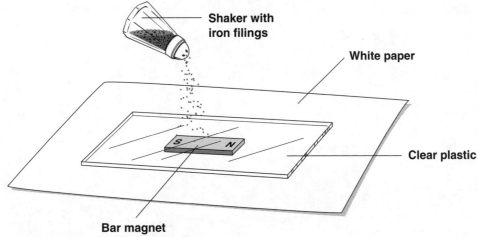

Shaker with iron filings

White paper

Clear plastic

Bar magnet

▲ **Figure 1** Sprinkle iron filings on a piece of plastic.

❑ **3.** **OBSERVE:** Observe the pattern of the filings. Draw arrows on Diagram 1 on page 102 to model the magnetic field around the magnet.

❑ **4.** Remove the top of the shaker holding the iron filings. Insert a small funnel into the shaker.

❑ **5.** Set the magnet to one side. Carefully lift the piece of plastic and let the iron filings fall onto the white paper. ⚠ **CAUTION: Be careful not to let the filings fall on the floor or scatter.**

Concepts and Challenges in Physical Science, Laboratory Manual © Pearson Education, Inc./Globe Fearon/Pearson Learning Group. All rights reserved. Copying strictly prohibited.

❏ **6.** Make a trough by picking up the paper from the sides, as shown in Figure 2. Carefully use the funnel to pour the filings back into the shaker.

❏ **7.** Repeat Steps 1–3 with the horseshoe magnet. Make your drawing of the magnetic field on Diagram 2.

❏ **8.** Repeat Steps 4–6 for proper cleanup of the iron filings.

Part B: Magnetic Fields, Using Two Bar Magnets

❏ **1.** Place two bar magnets on the white paper so that their north poles are about 2 cm apart. Place the plastic over the magnets.

❏ **2.** Use the shaker to sprinkle iron filings on the plastic. Draw what you observe on Diagram 3.

❏ **3.** Carefully return the iron filings to the shaker, as you did in Part A.

❏ **4.** Rearrange the bar magnets so that their south poles are 2 cm apart. Repeat Steps 1–3. Draw what you observe on Diagram 4.

❏ **5.** Arrange two bar magnets so that the north pole of one magnet is 2 cm from the south pole of the other magnet. Repeat Steps 1–3 and make your drawings on Diagram 5.

❏ **6.** Follow your teacher's instructions for cleaning up your work area.

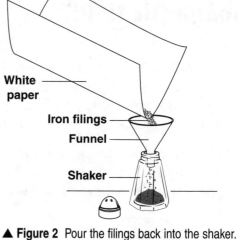

▲ **Figure 2** Pour the filings back into the shaker.

OBSERVATIONS

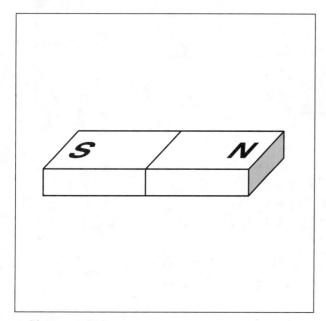

▲ **Diagram 1** Bar magnet

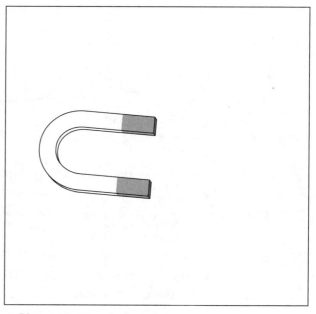

▲ **Diagram 2** Horseshoe magnet

LABORATORY CHALLENGE FOR LESSON 21-2 *(continued)*

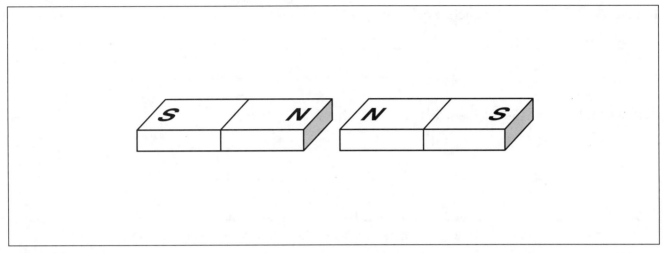

▲ **Diagram 3** Bar magnets

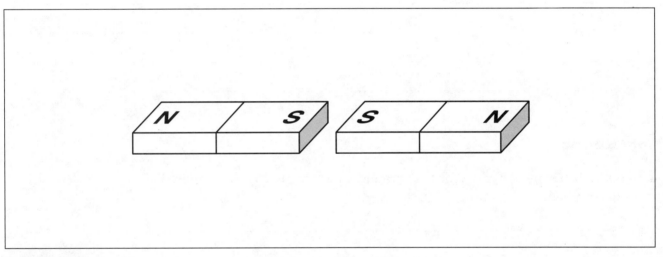

▲ **Diagram 4** Bar magnets

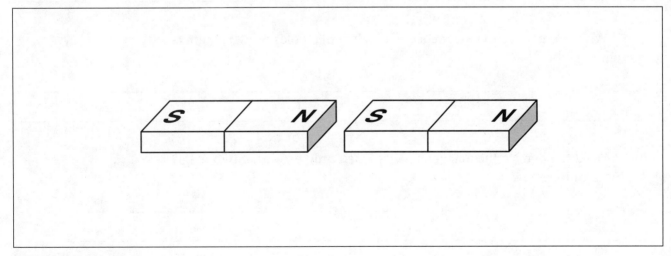

▲ **Diagram 5** Bar magnets

LABORATORY CHALLENGE FOR LESSON 21-2 *(continued)*

1. **DESCRIBE:** Describe the magnetic field around a bar magnet.

   _____

   _____

2. **DESCRIBE:** Describe the magnetic field around a horseshoe magnet.

   _____

   _____

3. **DESCRIBE:** Describe the magnetic field around two bar magnets when like poles
   are close to each other. Describe the magnetic field when two unlike poles are
   close to each other.

   _____

   _____

   _____

   _____

CONCLUSIONS

4. What is the shape of a magnetic field around a bar magnet? How can this shape
   be determined?

   _____

   _____

   _____

5. **INFER:** What happens to the magnetic fields when like poles of two magnets are
   brought together?

   _____

   _____

6. **INFER:** What happens to the magnetic fields when unlike poles of two magnets
   are brought together?

   _____

   _____

Notes

Notes

Notes

Notes